T0128144

IF LIFE GAVE ME
LEMONS,
I WOULD TURN
THEM INTO
HONEY

Based on a Life Story

ROSE SIMON

Order this book online at www.trafford.com
or email orders@trafford.com

Most Trafford titles are also available at major online book retailers.

Print information available on the last page.

ISBN: 978-1-4907-9798-4 (sc)
ISBN: 978-1-4907-9799-1 (e)

Trafford rev. 10/17/2019

www.trafford.com

North America & international
toll-free: 1 888 232 4444 (USA & Canada)
fax: 812 355 4082

This book is dedicated to:
Family & Friends (Old & New)
Doctors, Nurses & Physicians that treated me
&
An Extra Special Thanks To:
2 Members of the Biggest Boy
Band That Began in 1993

CONTENTS

CHAPTER ONE

Home Near The Graveyard:
What's Left of a Lost Past

A **girl should always remember her childhood.** She grew up having fun, enjoying life to the fullest, playing games, hanging out with friends, and begging parents for everything she wants. Growing up with more than one sibling should be a piece of cake, right? Maybe not, if both siblings are older brothers! Being the only girl should be simple, or so Rose thought. However, she often felt alienated. As well, when she tried to make friends, especially with girls, outside of the family, the friendships did not last long. She ended up hanging out with more boys than with girls, since her brothers always had friends in the house. Her childhood was complicated.

Occasionally, Rose would go over to her friend's house, across the street, to play house. She enjoyed the change of scenery, and the playmates, for a while. However, she found she lost interest quickly. It was just not her thing. Rose felt like she could not fit in anywhere. She did things she were sure were right, only to find out they were wrong. Could it have had anything to do with living beside a cemetery? She always thought people must think she was a freak. Did they think her house was haunted? What a way to grow up.

Rose's family home had a huge front yard with trees that grew around the side to the back. The driveway, on the other side, ended in a metal junk yard, hidden behind trees. A trail through the trees led to a little fort, and a trail that zigzagged through tall grass, behind the junk yard, led down a hill. Her father often followed this trail, to the town river, where he caught fish. He liked to take her there on rainy days in the summer, stating those were the best days for fishing. He was able to catch catfish, mackerel and pickerel, all in that same spot. It was a good fishing hole!

At the back of the house, the dining room had patio doors, leading onto a deck. The back door was accessed through a small porch, for added warmth in the winter. Also facing the back of the house was the bathroom and master bedroom. Rose's room was across the hall from her parents' room. She felt it was a special place where she could play by herself and take refuge from her bothersome brothers. In the back yard, was a basketball court with a difference: the net was on the side of the court, instead of at the end! Her father had also built a garage, much needed for protecting the family car from northern winter weather, since their town is located six hours north of Toronto. They had a comfortable home.

One winter she was on the roof of the garage with her brother. Suddenly she was sliding backwards, not knowing what was happening, until she opened her eyes to see only the sky, and heard her brother calling her. She soon began to laugh. She had slid right off the roof, landing safely on a pile of snow below. Rose remembers it, as if it happened yesterday. It is a wonderful memory, enjoying a fun evening in the snow with her brother.

Rose and her brothers did their best to get along.
The Nintendo system was a favourite pastime. The games always
seemed to have two opponents fighting each other, using martial
arts, or as they called it, Karate. They were into Karate stuff,
dressing up as ninjas, and goofing around. They even had a
pair of nun chucks, made out of wood and chain. Their dad
also owned an old sword that was only for show. They were not
allowed to actually use it, but even pretending was lots of fun.

Wrestling with her older brother was a favourite activity.
Usually he just wanted to test a new fight move on her. However,
there were times when the same older brother frustrated her
to the point she would run to her oldest brother, saying, "Kill
him for me." Of course, she was only joking. It was just siblings
having fun. The oldest brother would go after the middle boy,
simply to make young Rose feel better. The three of them carried
on this way, the entire time they were growing up.

However, one time, it got a little out of hand. The wrestling
position she was in, was pushing her face into the floor, until she
could not breathe. She stopped moving, felt close to blacking out,
and wondered if her spine was going to breaking in half. It was a
good thing her brother noticed, and backed off.

They had many games that went along with the fighting:
Double Dragon, Street Fighter, and Mortal Combat. The two
non-Karate games she enjoyed were Donkey Kong and Tetris.
Tetris was a favourite since it dealt with strategy and using the
mind. Rose was so into the Teenage Mutant Ninja Turtles that
she would get up in the middle of the night to sneak into the
living room and quietly watch videos of the animated reptiles.
She was caught by her dad, when he wondered why there was a
light on in the living room. Oops, she needed a better plan! Then
too, Rose played her brothers' Game Boy for hours, even passing
up on watching Teenage Mutant Ninja Turtles. Halloween was
the time for dressing like a ninja turtle, of course. She definitely
liked a variety of entertainment.

Later, Rose's interests started to move on to other
kids' shows. She enjoyed "Sailor Moon". The Sailor Scouts'

outfits intrigued her, but even more appealing were the powers they gained at night. Another favourite was "Mighty Morphing Power Rangers". She always thought the boys seemed pretty cute, but she wasn't interested in the girls! Rose also became hooked on "Breaker High", about a High School held on a cruise ship. She admired the way the teens got along together, especially when a girl and guy met and interacted in friendship. "Star Trek" reminded her of a Science project she had done on the Solar System. Rose was gaining many points of view, from her television watching. Martial Arts movies appealed, not because of the violence, but because of the self-confidence, the self-defense and the self-motivation.

Rose recalls a variety of family pets. They kept a pair of rabbits in a wire cage beside the house, under the trees. She and her brother fed the rabbits carrots and lettuce. When the rabbits died, Rose and her older brother buried them in the backyard. The second pet was a goat they kept for its milk. Next a dog and a cat came into their home. One day, they heard a lot of noise on the back deck; a raccoon was attacking the dog. It was a scary moment, but turned out ok for the dog. Pets added richness to her childhood.

On a book shelf in her house was a set of blue books. One, in particular, interested her. It was called "Cycle of the Human Body". It made her wonder, even in her early years, about the human body and what it did. That one certain book would often be in her thoughts. Of course, she also enjoyed books for a child her age. She found some puzzling books in her parents' room. They had pictures, but she did not understand the writing. She wondered if these were like the words she heard her parents speak to each other. At first, Rose had no idea their origin, but then learned her parents were from Laos.

On days when her brothers were not bothering her, Rose would take her bike and ride through the cemetery, beside her house. She would go through the lanes on sunny days when she felt bored and needed air. Tales of ghosts and tombstones might have spooked others, but she never felt scared, just at peace, since it was a place where the deceased were put to rest. She knew the scary stories were fake.

On winter days, when she wanted to be by herself, she would put on her ice skates and helmet, and play tea party! What a neat combination of activities.

Rose attended Separate School. At first, she was scared to leave the house, but soon progressed to looking forward to class every day. She was sure that not only her family, but her teachers, could see a change in her as she grew up.

Initially, she did not want to get out of bed, or to leave her family, to go to Kindergarten. Making new friends did not even cross her mind. She remembers being scared of the ceiling vent in the bathroom at school, making it difficult to go to the washroom. But some happy times in Kindergarten included hearing the story of "E.T. The Extraterrestrial", looking for her nametag on the pin board, being picked to say what day it was on the calendar, playing house, and playing in the sandbox at recess.

As she entered Grade One, Rose began to wonder about making new friends. She noticed her brothers were able to do it easily. For her, though, it seemed like when it came to greeting someone new, she did not know how to put the words together. However, she enjoyed doing school assignments. She even asked her parents if they were proud of her, for her schoolwork and work around the house. Rose enjoyed straightening out her dresser drawers, and did the same with her parents' dressers. Then she began asking her dad what certain words would be in their native Laotian language. She was definitely enjoying her learning experiences.

In Grade Two, Rose found joy in an assignment where she had to write down new facts about a certain animal. Then her teacher assigned journals, and she learned how to record her weekend events. Her love of writing was beginning.

Her family moved from near the graveyard, to a house down the street from the school. At the same time, she entered Grade Three. Her lack of confidence seemed to return, although she had fun doing word comprehension assignments. Unfortunately, on the last day of school, her teacher informed her she had to repeat Grade Three. She truly did not know what to think of the news. She felt ashamed and sad, but she took the news with her and decided to do her best to deal with it.

During Rose's childhood, she noticed her mother doing a lot of travelling. Her mother was into a home based business, constantly getting other people interested in joining the business. Soon Rose was asked to help with copying and filing. She remembers having to go down the road to some stranger's house and asking to use their photocopier. When she returned to her house, she stapled together these lists of items for purchase. Her mom called in orders, which were delivered to their door. People then came and picked up their orders. Her mom began talking about having a big dream, going places, experiencing having freedom. Rose recalls seeing tapes showing people who had already begun living their dream. They motivated her mom to work even harder.

One day, her mom was out with a friend. Rose was having her bath. Everything was fine until she called her dad, in English, and in her family's native language, to tell him she was done. Finally her dad came in. He told her to stand up and he grabbed the soap. She noticed how roughly he was washing her. She felt pain. She blacked out and woke up in the hospital. The next thing she remembered was being in a hospital bathroom, with her mom telling her to pee in a cup. It was not a nice experience.

One time, when Rose was about nine years old, she and her mother were in a coffee shop at the mall. Her mother was getting to know someone, in order to introduce her to the business. Rose became bored and wandered off, without telling her mom. She went into the nail salon that was next door and began a conversation with one of the employees. Rose hoped to interest the woman in her mom's business. It was not long before her mom came looking and found her talking. Her mom quickly took down the person's contact info. Rose noticed that her mom was excited. All the way home, her mom could not stop talking about how happy she was to have the contact info for the woman that worked at the nail salon. Rose felt happy that she was able to help out, or so she thought.

Once they were home, she watched her mom get all hyped with sharing that she got a contact at the mall. Rose kept waiting for her mom to say, "Guess who helped me get the contact? Rose! I found her talking to a person who works at the nail salon...." Rose wanted to step forward, feeling good that she would receive credit for helping out. It never happened. She waited, hoping for some validation, only to receive nothing.

So she did the only thing she could. She blurted out, "Yeah, I helped out", with a confident smile.

All she heard, in return, was her mom saying, "Go to bed." Rose just looked at her mom, the confidence and colour draining from her face. Her mom merely turned back and continued sharing about the contact, not concerned with Rose's feelings.

Rose looked at the person her mom was talking to, hoping they would notice the hurt look on her face and come to her rescue by commenting, "It is good that you were able to help, keep up the good work." But it never happened. Rose turned for her bedroom, turned around and took one last look at her mom, silently sniffling in hurt, and then continued to her room. She cried herself to sleep that night.

At that point, Rose was not sure if following her mom into the business was a good idea, knowing she would not be acknowledged for good work. She decided to do only what she was told, but it would be with a heavy heart.

Instead of setting the atmosphere to encourage Rose's efforts, her mom ended up taking over and pushing Rose into the shadows. Rose could not help but wonder, "What did I do wrong?" She figured that warming up the person, at the nail shop, was a good idea. It turned out her mom had not noticed and had not even realized her reaction would have a lasting effect on Rose. She watched as her brothers got involved with their mom in the various aspects of the business. They even suggested she be the secretary by doing the copying and filing. But it did not help.

There was the time when her family had company and Rose wanted something. She went to her dad instead of her mom. The response was the same! After trying to get his attention for five minutes, she gave up. She wondered, "Is it my fault I came into the world?" That is how she felt when both her parents ignored her.

Later Rose was introduced to Jane, a babysitter who made a difference in her life. She was actually the mother of the babysitter who had looked after her brothers. Jane gave her the attention she so needed and it made her happy. Being the youngest of three children, pushed into the shadows by her mom, and unacknowledged by her father, often made life hard. Jane's care was wonderful.

One time, Rose wanted to contact Jane, only to find out Jane had gone on a trip. Several days later, she grabbed the phone book, turned to the first page and dialed the first person on the list. "Hi, I'm Rose, Jane's granddaughter. I was wondering if you knew where she went." No response. Rose decided to dial three more people. Of course, she received the same answer. She was only a child.

There is one wonderful memory that tops all the rest: summer camping and blueberry picking. Her dad would get an old truck, and pack up blankets, pillows, food, and blueberry baskets. They would go out into the bush to camp for a couple of days. The entire family would pick blueberries, barbeque and have a grand old time. Once the baskets were full, her dad would pack up the family and head to the nearby fruit market to sell the blueberries. He always kept some so that mom could make her blueberry jam and pies. Delicious! Rose fondly recollects these happy summer family times.

CHAPTER TWO

Hometown and Barrie

T hen Rose's family moved two hours south into a three bedroom, upstairs apartment. All she could see from her bedroom window was the branch of a tree, but at least she was living in new place. She found it interesting.

At this time, Rose had no idea what her life meant. She felt her parents chose not to care about how she did things or how she felt, when they did not respond to her. She had lost faith in receiving help from her brothers, after they had not come to her rescue in times past. So she kept quiet about everything she did, when she was around her family. She figured her family did not realize how their past reactions had affected her.

She remembered a class trip for which she needed a parent to sign a permission slip. The trip was a tour of the inside of a prison to see what prisoners had to deal with, during their stay in a room with 3 walls and mechanical steel bars in front. Her father finally agreed, but it was quite humorous to see his initial negative reaction.

In some ways Rose adapted fairly well to life in a city, but at first she was petrified of taking City Transit to school. Talk about a new experience! In town, she rode on a school bus that picked her up at her front door. Now, Rose and her brother Jamie had to be at the bus stop on time, every morning, or they would be late for school! It was a big challenge.

Rose had always loved different types of music. Now she began learning artists' names. Her favourite hip hop performers included Sean Combs, Mase, Notorious B.I.G., and R. Kelly. In addition, she listened to artists her brothers liked. She then developed an interest in other artists, particularly ones that did not have the "f" word in their lyrics. Nsync songs really got through to her. She also became a fan of Britney Spears, Christina Aguilera, LFO, B44 and Five. The music was appealing.

One night, as usual, Rose was eating supper with her family. Nothing could have prepared her for what was about to happen. The sound of a person's voice touched her in a way she couldn't describe. It was like being confused and curious at the same time.

Her brother was checking channels on the TV. Just as Rose was reaching for some food, she heard a voice that made her feel warm in the pit of her stomach. It seemed to reach her very soul. When her brother moved on to another channel, she quickly asked him to go back. There was a music video competition. Her eyes were glued to the singer she had heard.

Rose realized she had a CD of the band, and in the days to come, she replayed the song "Everybody" repeatedly, thinking especially of the voice she had enjoyed. The band was "The Backstreet Boys" and the singer was Nick Carter, the youngest member of the band. She looked intently at the photos. She could not take her eyes off the mushroom cut blonde hair, nor forget the sound of that voice. Rose was sure it would stay with her the rest of her life.

Rose was too young to understand the meaning of the warm feeling she felt, when she heard Nick Carter talk & sing. She became curious, even though her parents had not had "the talk" with her. She believes, now, it was probably her first taste of 'puppy love'!

The uncertainty about where her life was heading, continued to be an issue for Rose. She remembered hearing her parents fighting, and often thought it was about her. Since her parents were Laotian refugees, she wondered if she should have been born. Maybe it was too much for her family. She was the youngest and the only girl. Rose wavered between wondering if she was an equal or if she was an outcast.

Another change came her way with the announcement that her family was moving again, this time further south, to Barrie. She informed her class and was pleasantly surprised by the response. She had friends who were comfortable hanging out with her, and who protected her from bothersome students. She started to become involved in their fun times and interactions. It was an encouraging sign in her young life. Of course, all good things must come to an end, and Rose had to pack up and move with her family, to the north side of Barrie.

In Barrie, Rose entered grade four in a portable classroom. This was a first. Also new, was being teased for her ethnicity. She was called a "chink". It was confusing and hurtful and did not help with her self-esteem. She was comfortable with the school work, but not with her cultural background. She felt alienated.

Something else took Rose by surprise. She began liking boys! At twelve years of age, she was a year older than most of her classmates, but that did not bother her. Her first crush was a boy in her class who wore athletic clothes. Maybe he liked going to the gym. It sure was a change, moving to Barrie.

At this time, Rose began making long distance phone calls to Jane, back in town. Jane had always seemed like a grandmother, during the years she had babysat Rose. One of Jane's children had babysat her two brothers, until the boys had witnessed some scary things that Jane's kids were doing. It

had caused family problems with difference of opinions between Rose's mom and dad. The reader will learn more about this, later. But for now, Rose found help in being able to share her day with Jane, when she was teased about her ethnicity or was scared by her classmates. For, in addition to calling her names, her new friends had discovered her fear of spiders, even plastic ones. Once they discovered her phobia, they tormented her to the point of making her cry. They used her fear against her. Rose needed to hear Jane's comforting voice. Her brothers made friends easily, in Barrie. This caused Rose to feel more isolated. Her only source of support came from hours of talking to Jane, often for two or three hours, before dinner. This went on for a long time.

CHAPTER THREE

Hometown Visit

Rose soon began to make trips up north and stay with Jane for short periods. It made her realize how different she felt when she was in her hometown, as compared to being in Barrie with her family.

In town, Rose felt like she could be herself, not being harassed or bullied. It made her hope life would be a piece of cake, being encouraged and nurtured with instructions for life decisions. In Barrie, she did not know what to do with herself, dealing with parents who seemed to ignore her and brothers who did not notice anything wrong. Rose felt pushed into dark shadows by the female, her mom, who should have helped guide her in right directions in life. It made her feel like a blind, homeless child left vulnerable in the world. Her entire family seemed too busy to see what was wrong. It made her wish someone would shake them and say, "Stop and pay attention to her!" Instead, she made an ominous decision to leave her family and go to where she felt good, safe, and happy.

In town, living with Jane, Rose blossomed, doing lots for and with Jane. Jane would acknowledge her actions, creating in Rose a warm glow of acceptance. Jane was like a role model, more of a mother figure than her biological mother. Jane had always been a mentor, even in the earlier days when Rose was bullied because of her ethnicity.

Unfortunately, there was an issue that Rose knew nothing about. Her family did not have a good opinion of Jane because of the way she had treated her own children while raising them. Jane had four children and her husband was deceased. Jane did not have the same relationship with her own children, as she did with Rose. This would cause problems with Rose's family, later. But for now, Rose was totally unaware of this potential conflict.

Rose had lots to enjoy during her visits in Town. She would visit her old elementary school, and update the staff with news of her family. She realized, too, that she had made friends in school, far easier there, than in Barrie. She longed to be treated with respect and acceptance. Then, when Jane taught her how to knit and crochet, she gained further confidence and comfort. She had a pink ball of wool that she used to make squares and circle, always counting the number of stitches. There was lots of satisfaction, being in town.

When in town, Rose recognized that her goal was to complete school successfully. The spoken voice that had claimed her attention when she was eleven years old and her yearning to be happy, made her want to finish school. She also knew she wanted to be someplace where she would be noticed, appreciated and understood.

And then it happened! Rose was able to stay in town for Grade Five! She had never felt better. She was back in her hometown where she felt comfortable, going to Grade Five at her old school.

Rose enjoyed her school work, especially English assignments in their workbook. In fact, she often got ahead of the class, because she saw it as fun. But this did not always sit right with the teacher!

Of course, interaction with other students came into play. Rose had the odd crush on boys, but nothing major. Bullying actually subsided because she was back in her home school. It was all good.

At Christmas, Rose was lonely enough to want to go back to Barrie to be with her family. By this time, they had moved to the south side of the city, into a three storey house with four bedrooms, a huge backyard and a two car garage. It was a great visit. Rose felt she would come back home, after finishing grade five in town.

CHAPTER FOUR

North or South?

R**ose's parents had warned her** that she could not keep going back and forth to town, and that the long distance phone calls were adding up. Rose was fourteen and was not too concerned about what her parents said, but she made the decision to stay in Barrie for her sixth grade.

On her first day she was mistaken for a fourth grade student because she looked so young! She quickly corrected the secretary.

During the year, Rose developed a crush on a boy and discovered he lived just down the street from her house, across from the school bus pick up area. When her friend found out about her crush, she encouraged Rose to go by his house and say hello. The problem was, Rose was not ready to do so. When she did work up the courage to say hi, Rose had no idea how to talk to a boy, even though she had grown up with two older brothers. The joy of teenage years!

Everything was progressing fine, until several students, including Rose, moved to another classroom. For the second time in her school life, she was put in a portable. She had to deal with some interesting situations in the new location.

Situation #1

That day, the teacher asked, "Where is my tarantula?" Usually, the plastic arachnid was sitting on the corner of the teacher's desk, near the blackboard. Nobody answered. Then, suddenly, a boy dropped it on Rose's desk while she was working. She shrieked and pushed her chair away from her desk. The boy removed it, but it was too late. Everyone, including the teacher, had seen how much she hated the spider. It could be a big problem.

Situation #2

There came a day when the teacher had to leave the room to be part of a photo with another class. He instructed the class to watch a movie until he returned. It sounded like a good idea. But Rose watched the same boy retrieve the plastic arachnid from the teacher's desk. She knew what he was planning. She eyed him with the object, praying he would not do it. She asked him, "Please don't".

He replied, "I won't". Relieved, she turned around to watch the movie, only to have the spider descend in front of her face. The next thing Rose knew, she was screaming and curled up in a ball on the floor, shaking with fear.

Immediately, Rose heard others in the class scrambling around near her. The girls were telling the boy, "Stop it! You are scaring her. What is the matter with you?" One girl took the spider and put it in the bottom drawer of the teacher's desk, out of sight. The teacher returned and walked right to his desk. The look on his face, when he noticed the missing spider, said it all. Having heard Rose's scream, he knew the boy had chosen to scare her again. Rose had to battle the fear for a long time, and wished she could change classes. She continued to experience bullying from the boys in her class.

Another experience involved her love of music. Rose liked the youngest member of the Backstreet Boys. It turned out that one of her classmates had the first same name. The class thought she had a crush on that student. So Rose played it up, by 'fainting' at her desk!

One hot and humid day, Rose was sent with several other students to go to her old class to ask for something. Until that moment, she hadn't realized that class did not have air conditioning. She noticed her old classmates were tired, sweaty and exhausted. Then she saw a familiar face. It was her old crush. Rose stood at the door, looking at him and feeling bad because of what he was going through. So there had been one advantage to changing rooms.

That summer, Rose's mother began working as a cook at a restaurant. Wanting to help, Rose began bringing dirty dishes to the kitchen. As expected, her mother responded negatively. "No Rose, don't do that." Rose sat by the kitchen door, not knowing what to do. Before long, Rose chose to return to her hometown

Seventh Grade and an Urgent Message

As her summer in town progressed, Rose knew she did not want to be anywhere else. She was with Jane, and that was what mattered. Once again, she was doing fun stuff with Jane's kids. They were all grown up and took Rose and Jane on trips. Sometimes, they took just Rose!

One day, as the summer came to an end, Rose was in her room, packing her clothes. She heard the phone ring. As Jane began talking, Rose knew she needed to hear the conversation. She went out and sat on the couch, to listen. Suddenly, Jane looked at her and said, "Rose, you are allowed to stay." Rose was wild with excitement, jumping up and down. She could stay! She did not need to pack her clothes.

Knowing that she did not have to leave, Rose sat down with Jane to make some ground rules. Rose had to make sure she used proper hygiene, she did her own laundry, and she did all her homework. It was a good deal.

Rose felt good, being back at School for seventh grade. Of course, she continued liking boys, too! At photo day that year, she developed a crush on the boy who sat beside her. He enjoyed basketball. Later in the year, she felt attracted to a boy in the higher grade in her split-grade class. He encouraged her to get involved in many things. Both were good influences.

Rose began preparing a speech for the Public Speaking in her class. She asked Jane for help and Jane introduced Rose to her friend, Eve, a retired teacher. Eve suggested using the alphabet as a theme. Eve did some research and they named the speech, "The ABC's of Friendship". After Rose presented to the class, the first thing she heard was her crush saying, "Rose, you should really enter the Public Speaking Competition." What an encouragement. At first, she didn't know how to respond. Rose noticed others agreeing with him, so she consented. She had no clue what it involved, other than memorizing your speech.

At the Competition, Rose felt nervous, since she would be presenting to professionals, not just her classmates. She did her best, without any expectations. Imagine her shock when, several days later, the secretary announced to the school, "The results for the Public Speaking Competition are in. First place – Tabitha for her speech about animals, Second place for Shane's speech about cars, and Third place goes to Rose for her speech about friendship. Congratulations to the winners. The final competition will be in three months. Thank you and have a wonderful day." Rose looked at her class, in complete shock. She had not expected that!

It was after this, that Jane told her Eve had agreed to be her tutor, for comprehension, for the second half of grade seven. Lots of positive things were coming into her life.

So Eve helped her prepare for the final competition. Rose came down with the flu, but went ahead with her speech, doing the best she could, under the circumstances. She did not place, but had no regrets. She gained a lot of confidence by winning third at her school. Getting praise for a job well done was what made Rose feel good inside.

Besides her school achievements, Rose was becoming more attached to Jane's children and their families. She got to know Jane's two step- grandsons. Their father was dating Jane's daughter, Stacy. Also, Jane's son, Joshua, had two grandchildren, and her middle son, Mike, had a daughter. While Rose lived there, Mike had another girl. Jane's other son did not have children.

Rose enjoyed helping out around the house. A wonderful occupation was looking after Mike's bundle of joy. Outdoor chores were favourites, giving her a sense of freedom that she did not gain from inside jobs. Rose would mow the lawn in summer. She adeptly climbed the ladder to clean the eaves troughs in the spring and the snow, from the roof, in the winter. This winter job allowed her to look up at the night stars, while she was up there.

But even more appealing, was getting wood, in the fall, for the cozy wood stove during the winter. In the fall, Jane's sons would pick her up for a lumber run. She would help load piles of chopped wood onto their trailer. When they returned to the house, she assisted with piling it in the basement. The winter's supply of firewood was ready. And Rose had a workout without going to the gym!

Jane's daughter, Stacy, showered Rose with gifts and made sure Rose was included in activities with the stepsons. Rose remembers one gift that made her especially happy; Stacy bought Rose a CD of the Backstreet Boys Millennium. It had just been released! And it came with a poster showing the band dressed in suits. She would sit by the poster when she listened to the CD and imagine they were singing to her. It gave her confidence.

Rose placed a book order, in class, for the book, "Backstreet Boys: Backstage Pass". The day the orders arrived, her teacher informed the class there was an extra copy of that very book! But it turned out Rose was not the only fan. So the teacher held a draw. Rose entered, never expecting to win. When the winning name was drawn, guess whose it was? Rose! When the teacher put it on her desk, Rose was in shock. Imagine having *two* copies!

Unfortunately, all was not well at school. The teacher noticed her division skills, in Math, were not up to scratch. Rose did not know her multiplication tables, an essential for proceeding to division. She also did not grasp that subtraction was involved in the process.

Fortunately, her tutor, Eve, stepped in and made the difference. Whenever Rose finished her comprehension homework, Eve had her work on multiplication and division equations. And Rose got a delicious reward for all her hard work: homemade chocolate mint treats. Her successful learning and her yummy incentives went hand in hand.

Occasionally, Rose felt lonely for her family, but often, instead of calling Barrie, she turned on her Backstreet Boys music. Two songs, in particular, would help her feel better: "I Want it That Way" and "Don't Want You Back". The rhythm made her feel safe, protected and confident. She was never quite sure why. Rose seldom asked Jane if her mother had called. It did not seem to come to her mind.

Once, in the summer, Rose and the young stepsons camped out in Stacy's backyard. It was hot and humid. The young boys thought up games to keep them occupied. At first they were harmless, but then they began Truth or Dare. The dares changed from being friendly, to being x- rated. The acts went from kisses, to hickeys, to exposing private parts. Rose did not know any better, and it definitely got weird.

The next day, they were brought into the house and sat down for a serious talk. They were asked what had happened the night before in the tent. Rose was asked about the mark on her neck.

She had no idea until Stacy told her to look in a mirror. She saw a brown spot. Now Rose was really scared. A fourteen-year-old girl, being asked to do things like that with younger boys, did not seem right.

Nothing more was ever said, and Rose never thought of talking to her mom about it. She actually had no idea that her mom always called several times a week to ask how she was doing. Most of the time, Rose was not home, or busy with Stacy and the boys.

Stacy and her boyfriend discussed giving something to Rose to keep her quiet, in case she ever decided to tell her mother. So they bought her a bike.

By the time Rose was fifteen, she was very interested in becoming an altar server or a cross bearer at church. She readily joined in the training and the participation. Rose remembers one time in particular, when she felt sick, with cold sweats and nausea, right in the middle of the service. She managed to cover her mouth and not be sick, and was able to finish the service. Rose never told Jane about the incident. She wanted to continue serving in the church.

Now, Rose began to prepare for the Science Fair. She had to come up with a good invention. Her project was built using items from the tool shed. She called it a hovercraft. But, just as she was ready to present her project, things with Rose's family came to a screeching halt. She noticed her teacher had a grim look on his face. He relayed an urgent message from Jane that she was to go home immediately. She biked the five minutes home, in a panic. Jane met her at the door with the news her brother had been in a car accident.

Rose took two steps into the living room and collapsed in tears. For the first time since staying with Jane, she asked to call her mom. Her mom informed her Jamie was in critical condition and that Stacy and Jane would drive her the six hours south to the medical facility. Rose headed to her room in tears, to pack her clothes. She had no idea what she would discover in Toronto.

Jamie's Ordeal

Rose and Jane got settled in Stacy's car. Rose did her best to hold back tears, but it was difficult, knowing her brother was seriously hurt. She did manage to sleep most of the way to Toronto, but each time she woke, she found it hard not to cry. Rose had awful feelings as they arrived at the hospital. What would she find?

Her family was waiting on the second floor of the medical facility. As soon as she saw her mom, she ran straight into her arms and cried more tears of anguish. She noticed her mom's boyfriend, Tom, and her oldest brother, Bob.

Once Rose had calmed down, she asked if she could see Jamie. Bob took her through two sets of doors, while Rose prayed Jamie would not look too damaged from the accident. When they found Jamie's bed, they each stood on one side of him. Rose wanted to cry, but held strong, caressing his right hand and holding it in hers.

To Rose, it looked like Jamie was in a deep sleep. He had sustained a brain injury that had put him in a coma. His left arm was broken and in a cast. His head was in a bandage. Rose did not know what to say, so she prayed he would wake up without a lot of brain damage.

This accident put a lot of stress on Rose. Even though they were not close, they were brother and sister. He was just over two years older than she was. As they were growing up, they had had their fair share of moments and, of course, gotten on each other's nerves, as siblings do.

Then, her mom told Rose her birth dad would arrive tomorrow, to see Jamie. She was excited, because she had not seen him for a long time. She stayed the night in a hotel across the road, with Jane and her mom. As she entered the family lounge area, the next day, there was her dad. She ran right over, and gave him a hug and sat in his lap. Now, her dad had returned to his original vocation, as a Buddhist monk. But to her, it didn't matter that he was in his robe, he was still her father. Her mom and dad let it go, this one time.

Once, when Rose was visiting with Jamie, the nurses had him sitting up in a lounge chair, even though he was still in a coma. When it came time to put him back in bed, the nurses asked her if she would like to help. She stood by his head and on a count of three, lifted his head. She made sure his neck was straight as she lifted. It was important to keep it from further damage. She was thrilled to be able to help. She knew her mom probably would not think she was strong enough. But all those lumber runs with Mike and Randy, in town, had developed muscle and strength. Lifting pieces of wood, over fifty times a session, had sure done the job.

Far too soon, it was time for Rose and Jane to return to town. School was starting. Not long after they left, Jamie woke up. Rose was able to speak with Jamie on the phone for a few minutes. His voice was harsh from being on a ventilator for two weeks. But it was great to talk to him!

Okay, so now Rose was back in school. She remembered one project in particular. By that time, Rose was having comprehensive tutoring sessions with Eve, every day, after school. So, of course, Eve helped her with the project. When Rose's teacher handed back the project, he looked at her with a very serious expression on his face. He asked if she had help putting the project together. Rose hung her head. She had no idea how to answer. She was scared to lie, but uncertain if she should admit Eve helped her. So she stayed quiet. But it was fine. She had received a mark of 83%! For some reason, Rose had no idea what the mark meant. When she asked a classmate if it was a pass, the student looked at her as if she was crazy. Rose had to ask Eve for clarification. She was thrilled to hear she had done really well.

At the end of Grade Seven, Rose was pleased to be able to go to the dance at Grade Eight graduation and to dance with one of the boys she had a crush on. She even revealed to him that she liked him. He looked shocked, yet flattered. Later, she noticed another of the boys she liked was competing with another boy, for the attention of a special girl. She wondered if she would ever be caught in a love triangle like that. Wouldn't that be something?

Soon after the dance, Rose and Jane were able to go back down south to visit Jamie in Toronto. He had been moved a floor higher in the hospital. One day, Rose and Jane and her dad had lunch in the cafeteria. On the way back to the room, she discovered her dad was no longer with them. He had stopped to make a phone call. When they arrived back in the room, they could see that something was very wrong with Jamie. The nurse had taken Jamie off the ventilator and he was in distress. The nurse tried to put a mask back on, but he would not allow it to give him oxygen. The picture that came to Rose's mind was that of a big mouth bass, gasping for air. It was terrible.

It seemed to Rose that Jamie was in panic mode. Jane was trying to calm him down. Rose tried not to cry. Finally, Jane noticed how upset Rose was and told her to go find her dad. He was still on the phone! When he finally arrived in the room, Jamie was asleep. The nurse had given him a sedative. Rose felt like her dad had abandoned Jamie, when he really needed them by his side at all times. Her dad should have stayed with them, waiting until later to make the phone call.

Now it was time for Rose to enter Grade Eight!

Eighth Grade and Signs of S.L.E.

While Jamie went into rehab, Rose went into Grade Eight. Once again, she felt impacted by a Science Project and by Public Speaking. She was not nearly as successful as the previous year. For the Science Project, she left everything until the night before. Uh oh, that spelled trouble. She was supposed to research tornados. Public Speaking was a worse scenario. She could not get her mind on it, at all. It crashed and burned! Rose's year was not going well.

One positive thing in Rose's year was the class trip to Toronto. She enjoyed choosing a roommate. She made two choices. Unfortunately, one choice got into trouble with the authorities, and could not take the trip. So her second choice was her companion for the trip.

The class visited lots of interesting places in the city. One Rose remembers most, was the tour of a music TV studio. They watched how everything worked in filming with the camera. It was a good taste of what it was like to be on TV.

Of course, there was lots of interaction with her fellow students. A class trip provides more free time, than being in a classroom environment. One day, she forgot the key for her hotel room and had to have that problem solved. Then, she accidentally spied on her crush, as he got cozy with another girl from the class. Rose felt jealous, but had no idea what to do. Then, there was another boy who reminded her of her older brother, Jamie. He was into the Lamborghini Diablo, a very fast car. Interesting!

After the trip, Rose saw a new music video from the Backstreet Boys. It played on the entertainment news one night after dinner. The song she heard was called "Drowning". She could not take her eyes off the youngest member of the group. She loved his voice.

Other than the episode while she was serving at the church, Rose's health seemed fine. She took the risk of not saying a word about it to Jane.

Her mom began showing up to see how everything was going, during Rose's eighth grade. Rose felt happy and stressed at the same time. She did not think her Mom really cared. She did not realize Jane had been screening calls to protect Rose and had been telling her Mom she was not fit to take care of Rose, since her Mom was so busy with Jamie. Consequently, when her Mom came for visits, half way through Grade Eight, it was a little difficult.

One time, her friend from the Toronto trip was over. As soon as her Mom left, Rose turned into her friend's arm and cried her eyes out.

During her Thanksgiving visit, her Mom wanted to have a mother/daughter perm day. It made her happy and sad at the same time, because it still was not like other girls' relationships with their mothers.

Her mother came to her Grade Eight Graduation. It was an important event, Rose graduating into Secondary School. It was a pleasant ceremony, especially when her Mom witnessed her being awarded Third Place for Public Speaking. After, she had photos taken with her entourage of guests, including her Mom.

Unfortunately, out of nowhere, Rose began to feel herself overheat and loose her breath. She raced out the front door of the church, forgetting she was wearing two-inch heels. She tripped on the steps, and fell heavily on the sidewalk, dropping all her awards in front of her. She looked up to see her entire class looking at her. How embarrassing. Fortunately, Jane and her Mom came to help her up. Despite a badly hurt knee, Rose still attended the Graduation dance. It was interesting to discover that the boy, who had always snapped his fingers in her face, actually had a crush on her! That was how he figured he could get her attention! She felt flattered and enjoyed the dance.

Rose visited her family, during the summer. She noticed that she began to feel very tired, and was still limping from her injured knee. Her mother wondered if something was wrong, but Rose figured it was nothing.

Now it was time to return to town for Secondary School! Rose made some nice friends, including her first boyfriend. They were always chaperoned by his family. Whenever his family did something together, they invited Rose along. She soon realized his parents had known her parents years ago or so she thought.

It was four months after her fall, and her knee began to feel better.

Now she faced a new problem: bullying, in High School. Imagine! It started with a group of girls who chose to make themselves feel cool by bugging and teasing Rose. One day, she was waiting with her friend, beside the arena, for the friend's school bus to arrive. She would ride her bike home, after her friend left. So she was sitting on her bike, keeping her balance with her feet. One of these 'cool' girls picked up a stick and began hitting her on the head. Good thing she wore a helmet. Rose tried to ignore it, but finally swore at her and rode off.

Another time, as she was leaving French class, they pushed her forward in the hall, so she bumped into people in front of her. Fortunately, she kept her balance and they gave up, for that day. But soon, they tried again, commenting on how her hair looked like a poodle, and then pulling her hair. Next, they put a sticky note on the back of her head. But the teacher saw it and she did not have to walk down the hall without knowing it was there. Fortunately, Rose realized the bullying was probably because she worked hard on her homework and did not get into trouble, in school.

Badminton season rolled around. Rose practiced regularly with her best friend, who helped her learn the rules and point system. One day, though, when she swung her racket back, she felt her hand go numb. It was turning white with black and blue marks. When she tried to warm it up on her knee, her hand felt cold. She did not know if it was part of her previous symptoms, but again, took the risk of not telling Jane.

A short time later, her Mom called with urgency in her voice to tell Rose to get herself tested because something was wrong. Rose and Jane blew off the warning like it was nothing. Again, Rose said nothing of the former incidents. But as the weather got colder, symptoms increased. The effects were becoming difficult to hide. One time, while shoveling snow, it became impossible for her to remain outside. When Jane saw how white her hands and feet were, she immediately took Rose for a check-up. The local hospital quickly advised that Rose be taken to the hospital for more observation. More on the results later....

March brought exams and a huge change. Rose thought things were fine in school, but she was in for a shock. The Program Coordinator and Guidance Counselor called her to the office and told her to stop school altogether! She thought it was because she looked young and felt no one cared about her. That was not the reason, but she nearly blacked out from the upset. She wanted to finish school. But Rose chose to keep herself busy by writing a short story, about a friendship with a boy named Nick.

Then her step-dad called to ask Rose to stay home and look after her Mom. Her Mom was facing a serious illness and required care. Her step-dad worked full time in his own business. So Rose was needed. She left school, moved in with her parents, and began a correspondence course. It was English, on writing, right up her alley. Even though she found all the changes exhausting, she passed the course. However, by this time Rose's emotions were very brittle.

It all climaxed at a nice restaurant. They placed their orders and then her Mom asked her if she could eat all she ordered. Then her step-dad asked her if she was okay. That was it. She could not handle being around her mother anymore. She left the restaurant and tried to calm down. Thirty minutes later her parents came out with her meal in a take-out container. She went to the library with her laptop and worked on a novel, for the rest of the day and evening. What a way to celebrate Easter.

By the Spring of 2011, Rose was attending school in Barrie, taking local transit. She noticed an apartment building near the downtown area and began wondering if she could move into a place of her own. It would be nice to be independent and not rely on others so much. Another time, she was attending a Writer's Club at the library and began chatting with another girl who was in a wheelchair. The girl had Spina Bifida. Imagine Rose's surprise to learn the girl lived in one of the units behind the library! They went back to take a look and Rose tried to see if she could be approved to move in. Unfortunately, she did not qualify, but it was interesting to investigate. Rose was glad her parents did not know.

In the summer of 2011, her brother, Bob, decided to buy a condo with his girlfriend. He had met her before Christmas 2010. Then, Rose and her parents travelled to town for a fiftieth birthday party. She had brought a copy of her Published Health Story and said a few words about it.

Now the fall term had arrived. Rose was able to return to full time schooling. One assignment stands out. It was a report on how to keep an online image safe. Rose did a lot of research and received a Level 4 - or 100% - on it! It floored her! Another time, a group assignment on Stress Management proved to be stressful, with one of the members being very obnoxious. But Rose soon moved on to a history assignment on her heritage – half Buddhist and half Catholic – and received another high mark for application.

Rose accompanied her Mom on a business trip to Detroit, during that school year. They joined a group of business people on a bus to the event. Rose does not remember anything remarkable about the day, until she spoke with her mom on the bus ride home. Rose brought up the memory of the time when she helped her mom get a new contact and her mom responded negatively. Her mom replied that there was nothing she could do about it. From that point forward, Rose did not know what to think of her mom.

After this, Rose began to write poems and short stories about her family and her feelings for Nick. Many of these pieces were written while she attended the writer's club. Her mom encouraged her to write her father and ask him if he felt badly about the time when he hurt in the bathtub, when she was a little girl. She was able to write him a three-page letter explaining that the emotions from that time still bothered her. She received a letter from her stepsister, telling Rose about her stepsister's mother. It was confusing, because it had nothing to do with Rose. Rose decided to let it all go.

During her History Course, Rose faced a time of testing through another student, who had become a friend since the beginning of the term. First, the student regularly phoned Rose to tell the teacher she would be away. Then she asked Rose to switch places for the end of term assignment. Rose had planned on the two of them presenting together. Now she had to go alone. She worked hard over the holidays, but still struggled with her research and had counted on her friend playing a part in the presentation. Rose felt let down.

CHAPTER FIVE

Hospital

Jane took Rose to the medical facility. Rose registered for a hospital card and then they proceeded to a semi-private room, where a bed was ready for Rose. Once Rose was settled in, Jane had to return to town, leaving Rose alone in hospital, for the first time.

Rose had no idea how long she was staying, but she decided to make the best of it. She was free to wander around the floor, and to access movies and videos. When she had enough of that, Rose was allowed to use the phone in her room. She called her family first. She wondered if her family was even thinking of her, as she stayed alone in the hospital. The last time she was in a hospital was to visit her brother, Jamie, after his traumatic car accident. Of course, Rose never thought she would be in one herself, someday. Even though she had not told anyone of the former symptoms, she still figured she was in with flu-like symptoms that would soon go away. She did not receive much satisfaction from her call home, so she ended her day with a warm conversation with Jane, in town.

Then Rose laid down, facing the window and hoping that tomorrow she would be back in her room at Jane's listening to the Backstreet Boys. She began to cry, silently, as her mind whirled between family and Jane, moving between feeling brave and being petrified.

In her mind, Rose thought of Jane as family. She was unsure of her own family, feeling like they didn't bother to try to understand her, or to reveal the dark secrets from their past experiences with Jane and her kids. In Rose's mind, Jane was a positive aspect, in every way. Unfortunately, her family did not feel the same, but Rose knew nothing of this.

In the morning, after a night of fitful sleep, as Rose washed up, she heard Jane and Stacy arrive. They had brought her a suitcase full of clothes, so she quickly selected clean clothes to put on. They watched a movie together, while they waited.

Soon a nurse and two paramedics came into the room with a stretcher. It was Rose's first time seeing a stretcher so she walked curiously around it. One of the paramedics asked if she would like a ride. Rose climbed on, admiring the view from several feet off the ground! Jane was close beside her.

Imagine Rose's surprise when she was wheeled outside to a medical helicopter! Jane sat in a seat beside her and then the medics hopped in. Several hours later, Rose and Jane were shown to a room with a bed and a cot, in another hospital. She had been flown to Toronto! She was sure glad to have Jane with her. She didn't even think of her family.

The Evil Cocktail

Rose and Jane were introduced to the nurse who would be caring for her. That evening the nurse brought a 'k-dish' (kidney-shaped dish) and some mystery packages. Rose watched with intrigue. The nurse got a styrofoam cup and poured in the first package. She then poured in the contents of a cylinder, and mixed them together. Then Rose had to drink. She immediately spit the first sip into the k-dish. Her first thought was, 'cement', as her tongue reacted to the texture. Her nurse told Rose she would keep making it over, until Rose drank it all. So Rose resigned herself to beginning again. This time she took a big mouthful, but couldn't swallow it! Jane told her to not think about, just do it. Finally the cup was empty.

It took awhile for her stomach to settle down, but Rose managed to keep the horrible concoction down. She was soon rewarded by a visit from Stacy. As usual, Stacy came bearing gifts. Wonderful gifts! She brought Rose a poster of *Nsync and album of the Backstreet Boys newest hit. Rose beamed. It had been two whole days without listening to their music!

That evening, Jane slept on the cot beside Rose. Soon Rose began to feel terrible pain in her abdomen. She tried to get comfortable, but the pain got worse. She raced for the bathroom, to be sick, only to discover she had diarrhea! After that, she was able to sleep the rest of the night.

After breakfast the next morning, the nurse returned with a different concoction! Before long, there had been twenty two new concoctions, mostly to be taken before bed time.

One evening, Rose's mom came to visit. Rose could tell her mom was scared and fighting back tears. It was too early to have any answers about Rose's health.

Next Rose was introduced to a male doctor. He came with two med students, to give her a physical. From that point on, the doctor was present to help her, at all procedures. That first day, when they met, they exchanged big flirtatious grins and became good friends. This was very helpful. After all, Rose was 16 and supposed to be hanging out with friends and listening to music. Instead she was being treated like a guinea pig in an adult hospital in Toronto.

Whenever her family came to visit, there was a lot of awkward silence, as everyone avoided talking. It was difficult watching Jane and her family avoid eye contact. But, her family always brought gifts and took lots of photos. They would bring wonderful 'outside' food, to give her a rest from hospital food, and she often went for a walk with her mom, around her floor.

Scary Body Changes

In the second week, Rose could feel her body changing. She lost all appetite, even for her favourite meal: lasagna made with layers of pasta, mozzarella cheese, tomato sauce, beef, and parmesan cheese, baked to perfection. Rose realized it was the medications, causing nausea and diarrhea.

Soon, her energy level dropped too. Even getting her weight checked required sitting on a chair, rather than standing. When she finally looked in a mirror, she was shocked. Her face had become round like a chipmunk. What were the meds doing to her? She had always admired her slim, smiling face. Where had it gone? In the shower, she could no longer see her feet! Her weight had escalated from 100 pounds to 167 pounds. She had to wear an old woman's type of nightie, instead of pajamas. Rose even had to wear stockings on her legs, to keep her blood circulating.

Unbeknownst to Rose, Stacy and Jane were calling her mom and telling her, she was unfit to care for Rose. Her mom was extremely busy with her brother Jamie, who had just been in an extremely serious car accident. He was in the backseat and a telephone pole had come through and hit him in the head. Things between Jane's family and Rose's family were getting out of hand, but Rose was still unaware.

Later that week, as Rose finished washing up for the night, she stood in front of the mirror, and felt unable to move. She called for Jane, who came in and hugged her, assuring her everything would be all right. The next time Rose had to take the mixed powdery medication that tasted like cement, she asked Jane to get apple sauce. That helped a lot, as long as she did not let the medication sit in her mouth and become hard. Jane was a tremendous support.

Heads Up/Warning

One day at the end of the second week, Rose and Jane were sitting in a lounge area, near Rose's room, having a chat about this and that. A few minutes later Rose's mom and her boyfriend arrived to visit. Her mom sat in a lounge chair that was in front of her. Up to this point, Rose and Jane had not discussed where she would live, once she was released from the hospital.

Her mom began talking by stating how seriously sick Rose was, and that she needed to live with her mom. In a panic, Rose looked at Jane; she still had school to finish. Jane said it was up to Rose where she wanted to live. Rose looked at her mom, telling her she wanted to stay with Jane. Her mom's response was to warn her that she would be dead in less than a month, if she did not do exactly what Jane told her.

This brought a tumult of emotions to Rose. Her mother hadn't cared about Rose helping with her business, all those years ago when she was a child. Now she was predicting the end of her life. This many years later, her mom was suddenly expecting Rose to accept her guidance. Rose felt mad and upset. She got up, with Jane's help, grabbed Jane's hand and raced towards her room. They made it partway, before Rose had to stand against the wall, gasping for breath. Jane leaned in beside her to encourage her that everything would be fine once they were back in town together, despite her mother trying to curse her.

Jane and Stacy made plans to take Rose to town without her mom knowing, on the day of her discharge. Stacy showed up with new clothes for her to wear, black corduroy pants, white tight leggings, a thick cotton beige sweater, socks and slip-on running shoes. As she was putting them on, her mother and Jamie arrived. Jane, Stacy and her mom stepped out into the hall and had a fight over where she was to live. Rose felt anger building over the time her mom had been spending with Jamie since his accident. She walked over and slapped him across the face!

Meanwhile, the three ladies had been hurling accusations around.

"Where are you taking my daughter? Khem asked in anger.

"Mom is taking her back to town," Stacy replied.

"I'll take care of her, Khem, everything will be fine," added Jane.

"Why don't you let me take her home? I live only forty-five minutes away. If something bad happens to Rose, it'll take forever for you to fly her back here," Khem argued frantically.

"Why did you tell Rose she will be dead in less than a month?" Stacy asked in wonder.

"How do you know I said that?" Khem demanded.

"Mom tells me everything," answered Stacy.

"I said it because I know that's what will happen if she stays with your mother," Khem stated in defiance.

"You are such an unfit parent, as well as having enough on your hands with Jamie..... We will take care of Rose," responded Jane.

Rose's mom had had enough. She went back into the room, just in time to hear the loud smack on Jamie's face.

"Let's go Jamie, we will come back later," Khem said in a hurried tone.

"Why, what's wrong mom?" Jamie asked in confusion.

"Let's go home, I can't be here right now," Khem replied, taking Jamie and leaving.

Immediately, Jane and Stacy packed up for Rose, signed the discharge papers and called a cab. As she stepped outside for the first time in two week, Rose noticed how different everything felt for her, with the drastic weight gain. She said what she hoped was her final good bye to the hospital and headed for the train station, back to town with Jane. She was relieved.

Deteriorating Health

In the comfort of the train, Rose began to think of how her life had changed, now, with the extreme weight gain. When her legs became uncomfortable, Jane told her to remove the leggings, and she felt better, for a while. It was about a nine-hour trip, north. How would she handle the cold and snow on a February day, when they arrived in town? How would she walk to the car? It was all a new challenge.

But eventually they were home and although Rose was exhausted, she was happy. Jane had to help her into the car and out of the car, and then help her sit in the first available dining room chair, while she went back out to get the luggage. Rose's first feeling was that her normal life had faded away, her regular self was gone. Even though she was glad to be home, her questions about the future petrified her.

Jane and Rose had to adjust their daily schedules. Rose's body change affected everything. Normally, Rose looked after her own hygiene when she got out of bed, made her own breakfast and lunch, and went off to school. Or she watched TV, or contacted friends and went out with them. Now, Jane had to help her check her weight, every day, before the daily medication and before breakfast. Stacy's visits became the highlight of her day. Stacy's pampering and visits were wonderful.

Rose had problems with her appetite. Sometimes things were fine, but often they were not. She never knew when she would vomit up her meal. One day, Jane encouraged her to exercise. She began to walk around the house, but before long, she lost her lunch. After that, Rose decided she was not going to take her powdery meds any more. Jane called Stacy in a panic. The end result, Jane packed up Rose's things, and Rose went to live with Stacy. Jane needed a break.

Stacy's house was across the street from Rose's childhood house, across the tracks. Rose was now living in fear. She tried to take her meds, but knowing that Jane was scared & upset with her. Rose's health was deteriorating and she had no idea what to do. She had to leave Jane, take a daily evil cocktail and watch the scary body change. What could she do differently?

Rose continued to go to school as often as she could. On a day when she could not get out of bed, her best friend would often visit. Rose knew she felt like she was watching Rose change before her eyes. Rose felt the same way.

Attempted Suicide

One evening while Rose was lying in bed, she felt herself slipping into oblivion. So she began to plan her suicide.

In Rose's perspective, her life meant nothing. She had risked not telling Jane about any of her previous symptoms, but had never thought her situation would get to this point. Her family's history with Jane and her close relationship to Jane all became too much pressure. Knowing her own health and life was at stake; Rose did not care about her family in Barrie, or about Jane. She just wanted to end her life.

Rose had two thoughts: break an arm off her glasses and stab it into her chest, or, get a sharp knife from the kitchen and stab it into her chest.

Jane actually came into Rose's room just then to check on her. Jane must have had an idea how badly Rose was feeling. She told Rose she was going to have a shower, asking Rose if she would be okay. Rose assured Jane she was fine.

After Rose heard the water running, she broke the arm off her expensive glasses and tried to push it into her chest. Her slippery hands would not push hard enough. So she rushed to the kitchen, opening the kitchen drawer where the sharp knives were kept. As she tried to push hard on the handle, Jane rushed in, with her towel wrapped around her, Jane took the knife and held Rose close. Rose wept in pain, frustration and hopelessness.

Seizures / Coma

Jane replaced Rose's broken glasses, and then took her to the local hospital for more tests. Rose was already delirious, speaking nonsense, and not acting like herself. Next, Rose went into convulsions, but, later, did not remember. Her last memory was sitting in the waiting room.

When they returned to Jane's house, they received a phone call from the doctor in Toronto, telling them to return immediately. Jane and Stacy called emergency services to book a flight. Rose remembers the first of the flight, but she soon dropped into unconsciousness.

During the flight, Jane filled out information papers, writing her own name as Rose's parent. This caused confusion upon their arrival, especially when Rose continued to have numerous seizures throughout the day, often calling for her mom.

Finally, at midnight, Jane called her mom.

> Khem: Hello?
> Jane: Khem, it's Jane.
> Khem: Jane, how is Rose?
> Jane: She is really sick, you need to come.
> Khem: Where are you?
> Jane: Toronto, at the Hospital
> Khem: How long have you been down there?
> Jane: Since 10 pm last night. Please come, Rose is screaming for you!
> Khem: I will call her father, then I'll be right there,
> End of conversation

Khem then made two phone calls. She called Rose's natural father, who was living as a Buddhist monk in California. Since it was long distance, Khem used her credit card for the call. She told him to come up to the medical facility in Toronto, right away. Next she called Rose's oldest brother, Bob, in Toronto and he said he would go immediately to the hospital.

Khem then woke up her mate, and Rose's younger brother, Jamie. They dressed quickly and began the one-hour drive to Toronto. Bob met them at the door of the hospital and they made their way to reception. Khem was shocked that her name was not on the forms. She could not believe Jane would do that.

They rushed to the private family waiting room, and Jane told them the doctors were x-raying Rose's brain, because she had had many seizures. Khem was very upset that Jane had doubted her warning, when they were down before, that Rose was very sick.

Rose's father, Chan, arrived from California, in the orange robes of a monk. Khem and Chan went to see Rose, on the stretcher. She was not conscious. The nurse put drops into her eyes, then checked the response. She then frantically began pushing Rose's stretcher toward the ICU.

Khem desperately asked what was wrong. The nurse informed her that Rose had just slipped into a coma and hoped there was not more brain damage. She needed to be stabilized in the ICU.

Khem and Chan returned to the waiting room. Jane worriedly asked what had happened. Khem informed her, then spoke accusingly. She was angry that Jane had ignored Khem's earlier concerns, when Jane took Rose back to the north. Jane fired back with the reply that Rose wasn't happy living with Khem. They finally lapsed into silence, as they waited for further news.

For two days they all sat around, waiting for news of any improvement in Rose's condition. On the second day, Khem could no longer keep quiet about the next of kin on the hospital forms.

Khem: Why did you put your name down as being Rose's parent?

Jane: Because I was taking care of her while you were busy running your business and looking after Jamie.

Khem: Did Rose never ask if I called, or ask to call me?

Jane: No, she was too busy living her life, just like you were doing.

Khem: Well she was in your care and now she is in a coma. What does that say about you?

Jane: Well at least she was with someone who cared for her.

Khem: ROSE IS FIGHTING FOR HER LIFE!

Jane: I TOOK CARE OF HER!

Khem: SHE IS MY DAUGHTER!

Jane: WHO YOU DIDN'T CARE MUCH ABOUT!

Khem: I was busy.

Jane: Nice excuse, Khem.

Then Tom intervened. "Okay, take a breather and go for a walk, Khem. The others are with Rose right now. We can see that you both love Rose very much, but fighting isn't going to bring her back."

Shortly after this, Rose was moved to another floor. Unfortunately, she had another seizure that attacked her lungs, and had to be put back in ICU, on a ventilator,

Day three brought no change. The staff expressed concern about whether Rose would wake up. The doctor brought a priest and told the family he thought it possible that Rose would not make it through the night. The illness had now attacked her liver and her kidneys. There was nothing more that could be done.

Khem went to the chapel to pray. An idea came to her. She returned to the room to ask the doctor to put Rose on dialysis to clean her kidneys. The doctor said it was useless. Khem insisted and went to find the dialysis unit. When that nurse heard Rose was in ICU, she came immediately. They hooked Rose up. Now the waiting began again.

CHAPTER SIX

Waking Up

After the eye drops, Rose's world went black. Then she began dreaming; she could feel herself move her head but things did not look right. She was lying down and seeing people at the foot of her bed, but she felt lost in a place where she could not move or speak.

Rose recognized many things: her Mom's boyfriend, Tom, was visiting her, her brothers were there, her oldest brother, Bob was crying, her youngest brother, Jamie, had put his headphones on her, and her birth dad was there in his orange monk robes.

Then everything disappeared and she began to feel wet under her body. Because of the dialysis machine, the bed pad had to be changed. Soon there was no liquid left. Her family saw a girl who looked anorexic. It was a difficult time for all.

At one point Rose dreamed she was being gathered up by her dad, who was now in regular clothes. He seemed to drive to the end of the earth. Then she felt the van tipping and heard voices. Then Rose felt she was tipping towards the heavens.

The voices were calling out her name. A friend of Jamie's said, "Rose, come back". Jane's daughter, Stacy, said, "Rose, come back". Her oldest brother, Bob, repeated, "Rose, come back". Then Jamie hollered, "ROSE, COME BACK!"

Rose opened her eyes. She saw pale white curtains and a night sky. She had no idea the time of day. She began screaming for her Mom. The nurse came running in, then ran straight to the waiting room. Khem was certainly glad she had insisted on putting Rose on the dialysis machine. The first thing Rose said, as her Mom hugged her was, "Can you ask Jane if I can come home with you?"

Rose had been in a coma for three days. The multiple seizures had attacked the frontal lobe of her brain. Part of her memory had been wiped out – like a clean slate. Her nurse informed Khem that the doctor had booked her for a CT Scan for her brain. Khem agreed it was a good idea to find out how extensive the brain damage was and how much of her memory might resurface.

Khem returned to the waiting room to share with Jane, Rose's request to go home with Khem. Jane was very upset, but Khem insisted. The doctor brought the results of the Scan. Rose's brain did have activity, but it looked spotty, meaning there was no way of knowing how much of her memory would return. Jane asked to go and see Rose, but Khem refused. Jane threatened that Khem would regret it.

Not out of the Woods Yet

When Jane returned to town, many people thought of organizing a fund raiser. Rose's school friends also signed a bed sheet, with get well wishes. Stacy returned to Toronto, to visit Rose in the ICU and give her the funds and the signed sheet. Stacy convinced Khem it would help Rose to know that people thought about her. Stacy put the sheet up on the wall.

Rose was beginning to sit up on her own and to interact with people. She was now able to leave ICU and return to her hospital room. Her mom noticed Rose seemed a little off. She handed Rose a piece of paper and a pen and told her to write down what she wanted. Rose wrote, "I'm hungry." Until now her body was bloated from the dialysis fluids, and if she tried to eat, her stomach emptied its contents. Since being on the ventilator, Rose couldn't swallow, so the nurse tried a double IV port in her arm, one for food and one for medication. It helped.

It wasn't long until Rose was comfortable in her bed and enjoyed the signed sheet on the wall. She was also able to have visits, from family and friends. However, her mom began to notice that she was always upset and seemed to have setbacks, after visits from Jane's children, or phone calls from Jane. Rose would be disoriented and confused.

Rose's family had to think of ways to build up her memory and her relationship with them. She had spent much of her life with Jane. The doctor put Rose through some tests and they always came back normal. Khem insisted the root of Rose's setbacks was her visits or calls from Jane or her children. The doctor said that was not possible. Rose too was wondering why she was sick after any contact with Jane. Finally the doctor agreed that Khem could have all calls from Jane blocked. From that point on, Rose did not have confusion or disorientation, just smiles laughter and singing!

A few more things happened on Rose's road to recovery. Once Jane found out her calls would not go through to Rose, she packed up all of Rose's possessions and had them sent to Barrie. Then a nurse mistakenly interchanged Rose's IV, mixing food and mediation. Rose's arm swelled. So, instead, they had to use a feeding tube in her nose. It worked for awhile, but soon Rose began to vomit. The doctor then checked Rose's throat glands and discovered she would be able to keep baby food down! Great progress.

One time Rose did not wake up, even though her mind was aware of what was going on. Another CT Scan was done, but it brought on another seizure. Also, she was continuing with dialysis, and had begun chemotherapy. Since her mom knew Rose's hair would eventually begin falling out, she did Rose's hair in special ways, with a party tiara, and took lots of pictures. As the hair began to fall out, her mom brought different coloured bandanas for her to wear.

A childhood friend and her mother visited one day. They were close family friends, and were also going through a rough time. The mother was astounded by Rose's good spirits. Khem commented on Rose's positive attitude.

Rose's brothers always brought gifts, especially Backstreet Boys CDs. Rose would sing at the top of her lungs, to the point that the nurses told Khem they thought she could be a singer some day!

SLE – Having Ups and Downs

Great news! Rose could go home! Her mother gave her a choice of how she wanted to travel. Of course, she asked for a stretch limo!

On her discharge day, Rose went all over the hospital saying good bye. Her mom took pictures of Rose with everyone. On their way home, her mom picked up a fruit basket, specially ordered for Rose!

As they entered the driveway at home, what Rose saw almost made her cry. On the garage door was a large sign with streamers, saying, "Welcome Home Rose!" When she opened the limo door, Jamie, in a colour coordinated outfit of jeans, t shirt and blue paid buttoned shirt, with a yellow gold bracelet and ring, was waiting to welcome her home with a big hug. Lots more photos!!

Stepping in the house, after her long illness, gave her incredible emotions. She was well enough to be home! And she was not the same Rose as before. Her new life was beginning.

As she settled in, Rose decided to go through her stuff from Town. At Jane's she had had a princess room, all decorated in purple, with a canopy bed. Her room here was much different, but as she sorted her clothes, she accepted her new room. One thing she noticed, in her bags, was a business card, but she didn't ask about it at the time.

Rose had to be on a strict diet. It was low sodium/low potassium. Rose was also lactose intolerant. It was a difficult combination and it took her mom a lot of time to find the correct foods. Khem put protein powder in most of her meals, and Rose had a hard time adjusting to this ingredient. But slowly, it all worked.

Additionally, her bedroom was upstairs and she was not strong enough to climb them yet. Tom had to carry her up every night.

Then one day when they were outside on the patio, Rose began to get tired, so they brought her in to lie down on the couch. Rose could feel herself slipping away. When her mom could not get her attention, she called 911 and Rose was taken to the local hospital. They discovered Rose was allergic to the sun. Rose had to stay in hospital for a month.

During a later stay at the hospital, Rose shared with her mom what had happened with Jane's grandson, in the tent in Stacy's back yard, years ago in town. Rose actually had trouble saying things well in those days, and did not express herself clearly. It had been a game of truth or dare. Instead of saying, Things got out of hand", Rose said," They abused me". However, there had been no abuse.

Her mother called Family Services, and things escalated. Khem distanced herself from Rose. Rose was given the ultimatum: take Jane to court, or let it go and move on. Rose knew that even though she was sixteen, mentally she was very much like a child. So the issue was tossed aside.

It wasn't long before Rose had problems keeping food down, again. The doctor suggested putting a feeding tube in her stomach and Rose agreed. After, though, she doubted her decision and tried to eat normally. Of course, she could not keep anything down, so soon accepted the process of using the feeding tube in her stomach.

Then Rose discovered her parents were getting a divorce. She felt like she was floating. Her real dad was never around and her Mom was dating Tom. All Rose could do was watch, as her Mom signed the papers. Before he moved permanently to the States, her Dad asked Tom to make a firm commitment to look after Rose, no matter what. Tom agreed, and Rose's new life started.

The doctors were testing Rose's brain for short-term and long-term memory. Her long-term was spotty, and her short-term was yet to be seen. Next in the process, Rose was seen by a young lady to test Rose's memory. She gave Rose her name, her birth date, a list of pets, etc and told Rose to keep repeating them until her next visit. Rose did, and proved her short-term memory was returning. Rose took another positive step by picking up the wool and knitting needles her Mom always had with her in the waiting room. She began by making squares. Rose soon put these together into a blanket that she dedicated to her parents' business team. It was pretty rough. The second one showed considerable improvement and this one she dedicated to the Backstreet Boys to show appreciation for their amazing music.

Another battle Rose faced was long lonely nights. She often woke up crying for her Mom. It was difficult, being a sixteen-year old and needing comfort. She often asked why she couldn't be at the same hospital, where her brother Jamie was being treated. She knew she was not able to go to the medical facility for kids because of the SARS virus. Now, because her memory was returning, she had to stay alone, where she was. This was supposed to be a positive development? Really?

Then, Rose did have a positive experience. The doctor, who had admitted her to the medical facility, on her first visit, came to see her. This was the Asian doctor she had had a crush on! It was great to see him and even greater to hear his news. She was being transferred to medical facility for kids! Now she would be surrounded by a bright, colourful environment!

There were still difficulties with her health, even at the medical facility. First, Rose developed a raccoon rash on her body, making her look contagious. Then, one night, as her Mom was hugging her good-bye, in Rose's mind she felt it was a very angry Jane, trying to strangle her. This brought on a seizure. Even in the midst of the seizure, she reached up her arms, looking for help from someone. Even though her Mom had to leave for the night, she sat back down on the bed. Rose climbed into her lap and began sucking her thumb. Everyone was shocked! The only way Rose would move, was if her Mom agreed to lay down beside her. Eventually Rose calmed down, and Khem could leave for the night. After this incident, Rose was moved to another room, for more supervised care. She was still struggling with eating, so needed twenty-four hour feeding.

The next stage was nicer. Rose began thinking of school! She discussed it with a child care worker, and soon began a weekly class with an English teacher. Rose walked to her office for the lessons. It was a nice addition to her routine.

This encouraged Rose to explore her life some more. One night, when there was just Tom visiting her in her room, she built up her courage, and asked him if he was going to marry her Mom! Not long after, she attended their wedding! Of course, it was very difficult to return to the hospital after the ceremony. To encourage her, her Mom developed copies of all the wedding pictures, for her to have in her room.

Rose continued to have bouts of loneliness, but listening to Backstreet Boys music was a source of encouragement. Additionally she learned she could have posters on her wall. A worker came around with a cart of posters, for Rose to choose from. Imagine her surprise to find one of the Backstreet Boys in business suits! Up it went on her wall. She couldn't keep her eyes off it. Later, she found a magazine in the store downstairs, with an article on the group. More wonderful pictures. Her Mom also brought a magazine with an amazing picture of the youngest member. Rose loved it!

Now it was Christmas. Unfortunately, Rose's illness began to act up so severely that she had to be isolated. What a way to spend Christmas Day. She thought the day would never end. Rose was close to tears, when there was a knock on the door. There was her whole family, bringing Christmas to her! She had seriously wondered if they would even think of her, because of the years with Jane, and the mess around that problem. So it was wonderful to have an amazing day with them. Rose had not realized that several packages that a nurse had delivered to her room, with instructions to not open them until Christmas, were actually from the nurse's family! Bob told her to open the big one. Guess what? It was a Backstreet Boys game! Once all the presents and stockings were opened, the family began to relax and enjoy each other's company. Lots of pictures were taken, to be developed especially for Rose. It was a day to remember.

Foundation

Rose's illness began to act up again. She could not stay awake. Her Mom told her it was okay to go to sleep. As soon as Rose heard that she was out like a light. The doctors said she might not get better, but also encouraged her Mom to not give up hope. When she went home, Khem asked her oldest son, Bob, to write to a Foundation. It might be the one and only thing to help Rose.

In her deep sleep, Rose felt someone gently trying to wake her up. She grunted and the person began speaking, explaining they were from a Foundation and she was permitted to have three wishes. That woke her right up!

Rose knew exactly what her first wish was: to meet Nick Carter from the Backstreet Boys. That could be granted! Her second wish was to go and see her Dad, in California. The third was to visit her grandmother in Lao. Rose was told to rest, and they would see what could be done about her wishes.

Two ladies returned to update her. Her first wish was to be granted! With every visit, the ladies informed her of the arrangements being made. They explained she would be able to spend five minutes with Nick, before a show! She felt a huge surge of excitement run through her body. She could not contain her excitement.

Rose was also visited by the rehab specialist, to determine what process would be best for Rose. Rose said she would like to go to the same rehab her older brother went to after his car accident. Days later she was discharged from the hospital.

Meeting Motivation

Rose was finally out of the hospital! When she and her Mom arrived at the rehab centre, the nurses were surprised to see her Mom come back. After all, her son was not here anymore. Khem explained that now it was her daughter's turn.

Rose was soon settled in a room. Over the period of her stay there, she had a variety of roommates. Occasionally, she even had the room to herself. She had regular visits from her family and from the ladies of the Foundation. Nevertheless, she still battled bouts of homesickness and loneliness that bordered on depression.

Rose became friends with another patient, an Asian boy. She soon became friends with his family, as well, and enjoyed their company.

During one of her Mom's visits, without Rose knowing, her Mom asked the nurses if they could keep Rose longer. Khem was taking Jamie to see his Dad in California. The nurses were concerned that this would upset Rose. But they finally agreed to lengthen Rose's stay.

So it was a wonderful surprise when a huge black stretch limo pulled into the parking lot and she saw her stepdad and oldest brother, Bob, get out! It was just after her seventeenth birthday. They informed her she was going to see Nick Carter! And she was going to shop for a great outfit, first! Well, actually, she had a massage first!! Talk about being pampered. She only giggled a few times, when they found her ticklish spots. Next came a purple manicure, then shopping for the perfect outfit at The Gap, followed by a wonderful dinner.

Rose was in a daze. She could not believe she was going through all this amazing treatment. It was beyond her wildest dreams. And she was going to meet someone famous, as well.

After a small wait, at the venue, they were permitted to enter. Rose was in a wheelchair, to deal with the fatigue of such an incredible outing. She wanted to be able to take in everything around her. She bought some wonderful souvenirs at the merchandise table and intended to get several autographed! They were then escorted to a lounge area, before going backstage.

Then, Rose met Nick! He looked even better in person than on television. She found it difficult to breathe! She felt eleven years old, again. She did her best not to show how overwhelmed she felt.

"Hey sweetie, can I have a hug?" And he bent down to hug her! Then he sat down beside her, so closely that their legs touched. Then he asked if she had any questions.

The first that came to mind was, "How can you be so cute?" He wasn't sure how to answer that, so asked if she wanted anything autographed. She handed him his solo CD, finding the page in the booklet where he was wearing a white tee shirt, with the posture that said, 'yea I'm hot'.

He was given a marker but when he tried to write with it, it didn't work. Úh oh," he said, "marker problems." The way he sounded when he said it made her giggle. When he found a marker that worked, he leaned toward her and asked her to spell her name. He wrote, "To Rose, Love Always, Nick, Thanks for Coming."

Then he asked her, in a quiet sweet voice, "So are you going to be here for the show?" Rose felt her face get warm, then she wrapped her arms around him. Nick chuckled and wrapped his arms around her too. Then he offered a hand shake to Bob, saying "I'm Nick Carter."

Bob shook his hand and said, "I'm Bob, her oldest brother."

Tom stood up and offered his hand, saying, "I'm Tom, her stepdad."

It was soon time to head out, to find their seats. As they left, Nick stood up and said, "It was nice to meet you."

Rose looked up at him and said, "I read you are six feet tall, let's see the difference between you and me." After getting help to stand up, Rose looked up at Nick, and said, "Whoa, you are tall!"

Nick looked at her with a chuckle and said, "Yes, indeed I am."

Rose stepped up to him, putting her arms up and asked, "One more hug before I go?"

"Sure," he said before leaning down for her to put her arms around his neck. They had a long embrace, then she pulled him forward for a kiss. He seemed a bit shocked but smiled. She thanked him, as she was leaving.

Rose noticed a long line of girls waiting to meet Nick. They asked her what he was like. She told them he was very sweet, kind, funny and caring.

Then Rose realized she had forgotten to get the poster signed. One of the ladies told her it would be no problem and took the poster back to Nick.

The auditorium was filling fast. Rose looked for a spot by the stage, and noticed an equipment box with the name, 'Carter' on it. She asked if she could sit on it and was told she could! She was given a cushion and Bob helped her up. She sure felt like a VIP. None of the other fans were this close to the stage.

When Nick came on stage, Rose felt all warm inside, like she had when she first heard his voice in 1997. During one song, Nick pointed at her! All she could do was clasp her hands, close to her heart. Then Nick shared with his fans about meeting a special fan, and pointed at her. It made her feel good and amazing inside to know that he had given her validation during his concert.

Rose didn't return to the rehab centre until after midnight! She had had a great time, meeting Nick Carter of the Backstreet Boys. The show had been a blast.

A few days later Rose had her last visit from the ladies from the Foundation. They brought pictures of her special moment with Nick, and of other times during the show. Wonderful memories.

Of course, during all this pampering and VIP treatment, her Mom and Jamie were in San Diego, California, visiting her Dad. Jamie did not remember seeing his Dad, during his time in hospital. Rose did have a grudge against her Mom, for not being with her when she met Nick. She knew her Mom could never understand the full impact it had on Rose. It had really helped with her recovery.

One evening as Rose wandered around the Centre, she noticed some low-backed wheelchairs. She decided to sit in one to see what if would feel like if you didn't have use of your legs. She wheeled herself around. Then before she returned to her present moment, she looked around to get the viewpoint of being permanently in a wheelchair. It was certainly an eye-opener,

At the end of the month, Rose was told she had to have her last round of chemotherapy. Once again, she was returning to the medical facility. She did not know what was next, after chemotherapy. The only thing she could do was play it by ear, taking one day at a time.

CHAPTER SEVEN

Excited About School Again

Rose's chemo lasted three days. She kept herself busy with puzzles from the playroom, and with watching TV. She was to return to the Rehab Centre, but there was a virus going around. So Rose was going home instead! Her brother, Bob, willingly agreed to pick up all the things from her hospital room. She felt a surge of excitement run through her! It was the end of March, and she was going home!

There was one down note. Khem decided to get tested for the same thing Rose had. Her results came back positive. It was difficult news for Rose, but at least her mom's illness would not be as bad as hers was.

Rose spent the summer regaining her strength and enjoying being with her family, home from the hospital. It was wonderful settling into her room. She had not been in it since 2001. She had fun exploring things that her mom had stored for her. There were documents and items from her time with Jane. She also found a business card from family services. She made decisions about what to keep and what throw away.

One thing Rose found was her chalky medication. She turned the label away from her, so she did not have to look at it! A wonderful discovery was all the stuffed animals she had received in the hospital, attached to a long purple string! She explored her dresser, which had a large framed mirror over it, her desk, and her closet. Lots of organizing ahead of her!

Her visits from physical and occupational therapists were welcomed, since they helped her get back out into the world again. It also gave her someone else to talk to, about things she did not want to discuss with her family. She confided her plan for the future and her feelings about life in general. For a few months she had a feeding tube at night, and had to be carried to bed at night. She was working on gaining enough strength to walk up the stairs. However, her best therapy came from arranging her room, just the way she wanted it! Rose began journaling in a diary.

One day the therapist was knocking at the door of the house, but Rose and her mom were upstairs folding laundry. Rose yelled, "Come in", but no one entered. The knock came again, Rose yelled again, but still no one opened the front door. Rose's mom warned her not to go down stairs without her. But Rose decided to make slow moves down the steps, hanging tightly onto the banister. When she opened the front door and smiled, the therapist had a shocked expression. Her mom came charging down the stairs, reminding her of her warning.

Rose just shrugged and answered, "Oh whatever, I'm still in one piece."

Rose realized her Mom still had her business. One day Khem asked Rose if she wanted to go with her to a seminar. So that night, she dressed up and went with her Mom. It was great to be out of the house, and Rose did meet a lot of positive people, but she didn't pay much attention, because it was 'business'. However, she continued to go with Khem to seminars and functions. One in particular stood out, because the organizer was incredibly excited. He had become a millionaire through the business! But the highlight of all these evenings was the band, 'New Hollywood'. They played songs from the 70s and 80s. Soon, Rose could not wait for the next event!

Her Mom had many motivational books and CDs. Rose wasn't really interested, but remembered a CD called "Oh Harry", from her childhood. It did spark her interest.

Khem also continued to take Rose to her doctor's appointments in various locations around Barrie, ON. Rose was excited about her growing strength. It made her start to think about going back to school. It had been close to a year since she had been in a regular classroom. She wrote about it in her diary.

Being in Secondary School had its ups and downs. She was worried that she might be bullied like before. But she tried her best to make friends. Also she began to a have a small crush on the teacher in her Career Studies. Something about him intrigued her. She would admire him while doing her assignments. In Science, one boy sat beside her and helped her whenever she needed it. Another girl was also friendly. But as usual, there was the pest, a boy who continually pushed his desk into her chair, so she could not leave her desk. Of course, she pushed back, until he relented in frustration!

With everything that was going on, Rose began to call Jane, to let her know how much she missed her. She didn't think it would cause any harm. It was nice to talk, when her Mom wasn't home.

Rose told the girls in class about her health, asking them if they knew anything about lupus. She explained it dealt with the immune system and she had been diagnosed a year ago. She continued, saying that she was doing pretty well, but it had not been fun being in the hospital for a year. When one of the girls replied she would rather be in the hospital than in school, Rose knew they really did not understand at all, what it was like to be at death's door. She tried to stay positive, but the girls soon told her she was acting like a 'bitch' around them. So much for their friendship.

Another class, Civics, was about politics and government and really did not interest her at all. However, one of the boys did! Every day he would ask her to use some of her lined paper. She gave him her phone number, but did not hear from him, because he already had a girlfriend. Rose asked her about him on MSN chat. That ended awkwardly.

Halloween rolled around. Rose dressed in outfits of three characters at once: a nursing outfit, a tiara for a princess, and angel wings. She though she looked fine, but others thought it was crazy. She thought she had been invited to go trick or treating with the other girls, but they did not tell her what bus they took to get home. She had to call her mom to come and get her. When she called the girl, the mother answered. Rose began to cry because she wanted to enjoy Halloween with her friends. She did not realize how childish she sounded. She actually was functioning with the mind of a nine year old. There were negative repercussions from the whole thing.

It started at lunch, on Nov 14th, her Mom's birthday. Rose was sitting in the stairwell enjoying her lunch. One of the girls called her over, saying they had something for her. Rose thought that sounded nice. One of them was writing on a piece of paper, handed it to her and told her to go down the hall and read it, then come back and tell them what she thought, The girls gave her a harassment letter stating they did not want to be friends with her. They clearly explained that she was letting her life be controlled by her lupus. When they called her back for her opinion, she simply said, "I don't know." The girls responded by calling her a spoiled brat and accusing her of being immature. Rose called her mom in tears, asking her to come and get her.

When Rose explained the situation to her Mom and to Jamie, they both seemed to think she should have known it was coming. Her mind could not grasp the situation. From then on she ignored the girls, figuring her positive attitude was far better than theirs.

At this point Rose's health began to fail. Three weeks before Christmas she had to go to the Emergency Room.

She wondered which of the three things was the cause: her Halloween telephone call, the harassment from the girls, or her secret calls to Jane. Maybe it was all three. During her three week stay in hospital she sat long hours on the windowsill, wishing she was home. Rose told her Mom about her calls to Jane. Of course, her Mom already knew, because the long distance bills had shown the phone number. Rose wondered if her calls to Jane had put her in the hospital. It did not make any sense to her.

But then, Rose was finally able to go home, in time for Christmas and New Years! She was bouncing the front seat of the car, bursting with excitement!

CHAPTER EIGHT

Growth of Conscience
and Morals

R ose had met Nick Carter a year ago. She had not
expected to develop feelings for someone who was way
beyond her reach. At the same time, she was wondering if
she would ever have a relationship with anyone. Of course, she
was often forgetting she still thought like a nine year-old. It was a
difficult mix of emotions.

Rose had just turned 18 and was feeling lonely. She thought
of her family members who were cozy with their significant
others. She was the lonely duckling, hoping for love. Even at
the mall, she noticed boys who would probably be nice to know.
But immediately, a picture of Nick would pop into her mind.
This was completely illogical and irrational. Rose knew it was
not a possibility. But it seemed better than constantly looking

for someone. So she reminisced about her meeting with Nick, listened to his Solo CD and wondered if there was a reason she had met him.

In a used book store Rose discovered a book with Nick's photo on the cover. The title was 'The Heart and Soul of Nick Carter: Secrets Only a Mother Knows'. It was written by his mom! She bought it and began reading, only to discover there were two sections. One was filled with photos of Nick, from childhood right up to his success as a singer. These pictures became a huge distraction. It took quite a while to read the rest! But Rose was able to complete a quiz at the back, so she definitely had taken in all the right information!

Rose tried to develop interests in others. Devon Sawa from 'Final Destination' and 'Idle Hands' was an appealing actor, and so was Jonathan Brandis from 'SeaQuest: DSV' and 'Never Ending Story'. But neither could replace Nick Carter, in her mind. Then, at one of her Mom's business events, there was a guest speaker she began to relate to, in terms of his health situation. He was Mark Gorman and had spinal issues and had been through a lot. She began listening to two of his motivational CDs her Mom had at the house. One of his phrases stuck with her: "The dream must be bigger than who you are right now." Then he asked, "Are you going to get the dream and press toward that goal?"

Unfortunately, this spurred Rose on, to try to contact Nick. In the spring of 2004, she looked up a fan club address on the Internet. She wrote the fan club a letter, explaining how she had met Nick. She was determined her words would make a good impression and she mailed the letter.

A few days later, Rose was enjoying a good time, hanging out with her brothers. They were joking and laughing, as they walked to the kitchen. They passed the side table where incoming mail was placed. Jamie pointed to a letter and laughed. It was her letter to Nick's fan club, with a sticker that read, 'Return to Sender'. Rose grabbed it and ran upstairs, devastated.

Her smiles and laughter, from the earlier fun with her brothers, disappeared. She guessed Nick would never get to know her.

Rose had never told her family about her difficult times dealing with her feelings for Nick. She knew they would not understand. Now, she decided to try a different tactic, searching for Nick. She found different websites where she could chat with people from around the world. She was selective with the guys she talked to, not wanting to be lured out of the house, or kidnapped, or worse. One contact was a blind rapper from the City. They kept in touch for a while. But none of it led to Nick.

Stop to Recuperate

Christmas and New Years came and went. Nothing seemed exciting in her life. Also, the school year was coming up. Every time she thought of it, she felt tired and depressed. She wondered how she could cope with the peer pressure from last term. Her Mom knew right away what was wrong and told her she did not have to go back to school.

Rose did receive a phone call from the school, later in January. As soon as the speaker said she was from Secondary School, Rose remembered the treatment she had received from the group of girls. She does not recall much about the call, except that her voice did not show any enthusiasm for being in school. And that was that.

So now Rose chose to concentrate on recovering! Being in hospital for a year can take a lot out of a person. She was getting herself back to the normal shape of an 18-year-old girl. She began to build muscle and to look healthy. Rose tried to eat more food, although she still had the feeding tube at night. Before long, Rose ventured out to explore her neighbourhood.

CHAPTER NINE

Family and Travelling

In September of 2004, Rose's G-Tube was removed! It had been a long process. She had been transferred to an adult lupus doctor, who gave an approval note to have it removed. But there were lots of phone calls on the day it was to be taken out. Her doctor had advised her that she needed it to help gain back her weight. Normal was 55 kg (105 pounds) but Rose was only 45 kg, at the time. During any of her stays in hospital, they had substituted for food she was not eating, by putting alternatives in the tube. She needed the tube to be sure she was receiving adequate nourishment. They had changed the timing, though, so the feeding machine was not an early morning alarm clock! Finally, details were agreed upon, and the tube was removed. What a relief!

The rest of 2004 was fairly uneventful. Rose continued visiting the website and chatting with contacts. For Christmas and New Year's 2005, her parents decided to throw a dual party, to celebrate her year out of the hospital. She decided to get all dolled up, to really celebrate! After all, her only visits to hospital, now, were for doctor's appointments!

In the following months, Rose did lots of relaxing at home, and got back into knitting and crocheting. One project was knitting large squares, 20 inches by 20 inches, in a variety of colours. She sewed them together, into a blanket which she gave to the leaders of her parents' business team. Then she began working on another. Rose thought of sending it to Nick and the Boys. By now, she had downloaded most of the songs from their albums since 1993. But she soon needed a break, and set aside this latest knitting project, until a later date.

> *Dec 13, 2004*
> *Dear Diary,*
> *Hello again,*
>
> *It's been a long time since I've written. I am 18 going on 19, in two months. Man, I'm getting old! At least, people keep saying that. I've finished knitting a blanket and have given it to my mom's business friends. It was dedicated to our team! I am starting a brand new blanket, in a different colour. Oh, I have some new photos on my wall. It is an actor who died by suicide. I've been recording his show, 'Sea Quest DSV'. His name is Jonathan Brandis and he is so cute. He is a computer analyst on the show. I look forward to watching it every weekend. I've bought some new clothes. Today I had blood work done at the hospital. And that's it. Oh, btw, my hair has grown back in and I am able to put it in a bun or a ponytail. Oh and I visited two people at the hospital today. Anyway, I have to take my needle now. Ouch. But it's not really that bad, by now. Bye.*

Dec 27, 2004
Dear Diary,
Hello again.

It is the day after Boxing Day. I didn't do much, but I did have pancakes for breakfast. Oh, and I think I have a boyfriend. He is 17 and was born blind, so we both have health problems in common. Right now he is in a wrestling tournament. I think he really likes me. He says I was a very nice friend for Christmas. He feels comfortable talking to me. He lives in Toronto and is an underground rapper. That's been his job for 2 years. He had a girlfriend but they broke up 6 months ago. I even have his name and number and what his background is. We have been talking for the past couple of days. Anyway, I'm tired, going to have a nap. Bye.

Jan 24, 2005
Dear Diary,

Hello again. It's 10:53 and I am not feeling good at all. I have a cold and stuffy nose. Also, I am worried my boyfriend is not talking to me anymore. Cannot contact him. Oh, and I'm going to hospital on Wednesday, probably for a few days. Anyway, I am going to bed. Night

Rose's 19th birthday lasted for two weeks! Bob was out of town working. So, the first week she spent with her mom, stepdad and brother Jamie. Then, when Bob returned, he joined them to help finish the celebration! It was a nice long party!

For Rose's next doctor's appointment, her mom dropped her off, and took Jamie to his appointment at another place. Once Rose's appointment was done, she would call her mom and let her know. Rose would be in for a few days.

March 12, 2005
Dear Diary,

    I had blood work done on my right ankle and did it hurt! My breakfast was cream of wheat with milk and brown sugar, and a glass of chocolate. I managed to eat half, but my stomach did not feel well. After a shower, I rested. Lunch was tomato soup. As I was eating, a doctor came in to talk. I told him how I felt about being poked 7 times yesterday, for blood work. He said I could have a pick line put in, instead. (On Thursday, the 10th, I spent the morning in emergency, and for the rest of the day, could only drink ice water. On Friday, yesterday, I had soup for every meal.) Tonight I had puree carrot soup, orange jello and grape juice. Bobby and Samantha came tonight and we watched the movie, "Ong-Bak-Thair Warrior". It is gosh darn funny!

March 13, 2005
Dear Diary,

    I asked mom to bring in several things I need. Mom also brought a surprise. I love surprises! It was a light-up pen and writing book. There was also a multi-game tin board. I get my pick line tomorrow.

March 14, 2005
Dear Diary,

    My pick line is in, and Bobby is coming to keep me company until mom arrives. Mom is staying overnight with me. I'm going to try and stay awake until she arrives.

March 15, 2005
Dear Diary,

> *I am feeling very homesick. I want to see my cat, and*
> *Jamie and my stepdad. And most of all, I miss my mom.*
> *Just having her gone for a few hours, makes my lonely*

When Rose returned home, she felt a lot of mixed emotions. She wasn't even sure what they were about. Were they about Nick, about her mother and the business, about her mother and her stepdad, or about wanting her parents to get back together? She had played matchmaker with her mom and Tom, so she did not think it was the last reason.

One day, Bob brought her a book to read. He was going to test her after, to see how much she remembered. She read, "How to Win Friends and Influence People". Bob gave her 6 questions and she could answer 5. Pretty good!

At the end of March, Rose's mom told Bob to take Jamie and Rose down to see their dad, Chan. He lived in Milwaukee, Wisconsin. The one thing she remembers from the trip was how close a transport came to their car! Bob had to pull off on the gravel to get back on the road. They met their dad at his Buddhist temple, where lots of pictures were taken. Then they went to his house. Chan had married a single mother with 2 grown-up children, a son and a daughter.

One day her half-sister and half-brother took them to a basketball court to hang out and play some fun games. There were others there to join them. It was interesting to see the guys showing off in front of the girls!

Chan's house was a 2-storey, 3-bedroom house. Rose slept on the couch, while her brother slept in the only bedroom on the ground floor. Rose managed to talk with her dad about his feelings for her mom. He still loved her, but she knew it was not the same with her mom. She did not find out anything about how her parents had treated each other, when they were together. She remembered hearing fights, in her childhood, but since they were in Laotian, she had never known what they were about.

They enjoyed other outings. Chan took them to an air show. It was great to see the jet fighters perform. On the last evening, her half-sister and a friend took her to a girls' night out bowling event. It was going fine, until she let go of her ball and it went in the wrong direction! Fortunately there was no one behind her! The next day, they left for Canada. It had been a good trip.

April 27, 2005
Dear Diary,

I've been out of hospital for 6 weeks! And I met another guy at the last business function. His name is Andy and he is 15. I talk to him whenever he is on computer. Oh and by the way, I have been off my injection for about 3 weeks!

May 25, 2005
Dear Diary,

I just got back from Brantford last night and my cousin came with me. For some reason I wish she hadn't. She keeps telling me what to do, even though we are in my house. I am happy she is only here for 2 or 3 days.

May 31, 2005
Dear Diary,

I am watching an old Christmas home video Tom recorded, from 2002, the year I was in hospital for Christmas. Oh and I have a huge surprise for you! I got my feeding tube taken out 3 weeks ago. Also, I get to go on a cruise with my parents, and to go home to Laos with my mom, later this year.

July 24, 2005
Dear Diary,

I got the most horrible news from the Immunology doctor. I have a very low immune system. I am scared out of my mind. I hope I don't die before I am 30.

July 29, 2005
Dear Diary,

Hello again, I am doing better. My fever has gone down but I am confined to my room for a few days. Can't even hug my family.

August 25, 2005

I am at the store working. We took over the store 2 weeks ago and renamed it. Tomorrow I go to the airport at 5 am to go on a cruise with my parents for a week! It is all expenses paid, compliments of my parents' home-based business.

Sept 2, 2005
Dear Diary,

I am still on the Cruise Line. I have had a lot of fun all week and have made some purchases on the different islands. I've also had my hair braided. I have to go pack.

Rose's brothers could have gone on the cruise, but they refused to join in. She could never understand why. The whole thing was an amazing experience. They had no idea what they were missing, but it was their loss. Rose had a grand ol' time and it was well worth it!

Sept 28, 2005
Dear Diary,

I just made my first follow-up appointment with a business client to go to a workshop, so I'm happy to say I'm on my way to being a power player and business builder by next year!

Even though Rose's brothers missed the cruise trip, about a month later, her family came back together and they all travelled to Laos, north of Thailand. It was wonderful.

Oct 13, 2005
Dear Diary,

I've been in Laos about a week. They are 12 hours behind Canada, so I'm still catching up on jet-lag. Back to bed; it's 3 am here.

Oct 19, 2005
Dear Diary,

I have just had some awesome news. There is a contest, to win 2 tickets to see and meet the Backstreet Boys in person at a concert. Hope my dream comes true!

Oct 20, 2005
Dear Diary,

No news yet, the concert is Oct 26 in Manchester, England.

Oct 28, 2005
Dear Diary,

Didn't win. So I bought a double disc of their music. So now I'm thinking about the future. I am getting my business builder jacket ready.

Nov 4, 2005
Dear Diary,

Great news! My cousin just asked me to go to Florida with her. It will probably be in March, when tickets are cheaper. Hopefully the Backstreet Boys will be playing.

Nov 9, 2005
Dear Diary,

So bored in Laos. It is not easy being the only girl. We are having a farewell part tonight. Tomorrow we go to Thailand for 4 days before heading to Canada.

Nov 12, 2005
Dear Diary,

On a very roomy bus to Thailand. Lots of legroom, a back massage and a leg lift. I miss my room in Canada. I am going to see if I can buy 'The Hollow', a movie featuring Nick Carter. Then I am going to lock myself in my room until the Florida trip!

Nov 25, 2005
Dear Diary,

I am depressed because I sent a letter to the Backstreet Boys fan club and it was returned. I used the wrong stamp. My confidence went to the dumps; I'm so stupid.

Dec 3, 2005
Dear Diary,

I don't feel great. I just returned from a dinner and dance party. There was this really cute guy there, but he went after my cousin, instead of me.

Dec 23, 2005
Dear Diary,

I'm back with surprising news. I just met a guy on a website. His name is Ryan, he is the same age as me, and he likes the Backstreet Boys! He is from Japan and says he loves me. Merry Christmas!

Meeting Inspiration and a Good Cause

Rose enjoyed going with her parents, to their business seminars and events. Her mom's sponsorship had been with a business man who was all hype and excitement. However the next event was very different. There was no hype or excitement or music. She wondered what was happening.

In January 2006 Rose's parents had a couple over for dinner. They were in the same business and Rose found out they were her parents' new line sponsors. They had changed to this local couple. So things would be a little different from now on.

Rose soon lost interest in the business. She missed the excitement at meetings. So she decided to leave it alone and concentrate on what made her happy; music! She decided to try a different method to contact Nick.

Jan 16, 2006
Dear Diary,

I just had a fight with my cousin, because now she wants to go to Kansas instead of Florida. She wants to see her sister. No one realizes how much I want to see the Backstreet Boys. Is that too much to ask?

Not long after, she was surfing the net and came across a website for a charity for Lupus, hosted by one of the Backstreet Boys! Howie Dorough said his sister had passed away from lupus cancer and he wanted to raise money for the cause. It was being held not far from their town! Her mother agreed that she could go. It was being held in June, so she had a long wait!

During this time, her mother took her back to town. Her mom wanted to see how she would handle being back at Jane's, after 4 years. It was not a good visit. The minute she stepped in Jane's house, she felt as if Jane was saying she didn't want her there anymore. She was not welcome. It left her dizzy and nauseas. On the way home, she told her mom she didn't think she could go there anymore.

The next week Rose was able to meet Howie Dorough, also known as Sweet D. It was like a nightclub setting. When her parents dropped her off, there was already a line-up, waiting at the entrance. Her ID was checked and she headed upstairs where there were drinks, snacks and charity items on display. She checked it all out, listening intently to the music that was playing.

Rose then stood at the top of the stairs, watching people enter. She felt a tap on her shoulder and a girl in a black-strapped evening gown greeted her, introducing herself as Bee. She asked Rose if she would like to join her checking out all the souvenirs. Soon they were chatting like old friends. They even exchanged email and phone numbers, so they could stay in touch.

Next, Rose and her new friend joined the line for the mini concert. They found a seat close to the front of the stage, in the small room. The first performer was Howie D's protégé, George Nozuka. He was an attractive musician, talented on the guitar and keyboard.

Then, Howie stepped on stage, and the crowd went wild! When things finally calmed down, Howie explained about his sister, Caroline and the development of his Lupus foundation in her memory. Then he took them down memory lane, singing Backstreet Boys songs. Rose could list the songs and their albums. The song, "Drowning", brought back memories of being in the coma in the hospital. She silently cried all the way through. She hoped no one noticed.

Now there was a meet and greet with Howie. Rose and Bee waited to be last. While they stood there, Bee encouraged her to tell Howie about her battle with Lupus SLE and about how that one song meant so much to her.

Finally it was Rose's turn. She told Howie she was there for two reasons:

1.   She had been a fan of the Backstreet Boys since she was 11, and she had met Nick before.
2.   She had come to support his Lupus foundation because she also had had Lupus SLE, since she was 16, and had been taking medication daily.

Rose told Howie, that as soon as he sang 'Drowning' she had this image of being in the hospital room in 2002, when she was really sick. She hadn't realized how much the song meant to her. She remembered always singing along to it, in the hospital. She also explained how important the song, 'What Makes You Different', was to her. It reminded her of her days in high school when she was bullied. It had been hard to hold in her emotions, back then. Howie gave her a hug to help her feel better! When she listed the details of her illness and her medications, Howie gave her another hug, reminding her to always take the proper dosages. He told her she was a very strong person who could help and inspire others with her story. Then, they had their picture taken together. Rose thanked his bodyguard, and left.

Two days later, Rose sat down at her computer. She didn't really plan it, but she began writing out what she had gone through with her health. She wrote from her own point of view, and from her mother's. This book is the result.

Rose went to visit her cousin in Brantford. Her mother had introduced them during Christmas of 2004. She found most visits were depressing because her cousin would go on about the church and people with issues. But this time, Rose kept herself busy working on her second blanket. Since meeting Howie, she labeled the blanket, 'The Backstreet Blanket'. On the blanket, there were the names of all five singers, seven of her favourite song titles, and Howie's famous quote: 'Keep The Backstreet Pride Alive'. Rose also made a discovery, while on line at her cousin's apartment. Kevin Richardson was leaving the group. She was shocked that now, if she did get to a concert, there would only be four members.

A month later, Rose found a website called 'Myspace'. On it she saw Nick's profile. She joined and was thrilled to receive a blog update from him. She did not know, at the time, that everyone on the site received it. It sure left her thrilled!

In the second week of September, Rose received wonderful news. She was having a nap one day, and her mom came in the room, to inform her that the doctor had just called. They had cancelled her appointment of the 13th, because Rose had been clean for 3 years, and no long had to worry about getting PCP Pneumonia! Incredible news! Her Lupus SLE was getting better and better as time went by. She was still getting poked weekly, for blood work. But even that changed to every 2 weeks, because she could have a different injection to deal with a blood clot on her left arm. All that was left was to wait to see when her Lupus doctor wanted to see her again.

Then Rose had more good news. Howie was having another charity, this time in New York, NY. She and her mother decided to make it a road trip, with another friend, Brenda, and her daughter. They made it a scenic car trip. It saved money, not flying. At the border, Brenda warned everyone not to all talk at once, to avoid confusion. All it did was make them want to giggle!

They reached The Big Apple! It took a while for them to find the hotel since it was not directly in Manhattan. The next day they rode a shuttle into the city. It took nearly a day to locate the charity. It was at Jay-Z's 40/40 Club. Imagine their surprise to discover there was also a movie being filmed there. Then they noticed a car pull up and were stunned to see Will Smith get out! He was filming the movie called, 'I Am Legend'! He was one of her mother's favourite actors. Rose grew up watching 'The Prince of Bel Air'. Her mother rushed all over the place, taking pictures!

Since they were early for the event, they were given a tour of the Club! Then they were shown into the room where the event was being held. The walls were decorated with photos of celebrities from the 50s, 60s, 70s and 80s. It was fascinating. The room began to fill, with everyone waiting for the Host to arrive! Rose chatted with a few girls, and explained she had a gift (the blanket) for Howie. One of the girls knew of a phone number where she could leave a message for Nick! She dialed on Rose's phone and handed the phone back to her. Rose explained where she had met him before, but she left her email instead of her phone number. (Unfortunately, she did not hear back from him.)

Then whispers spread around the room stating that Howie was here. Rose could see him by the door. She waved and he waved back. Her friends encouraged her to go and tell him about her gift. It took her a while, but she finally built up the courage and walked over to him. She asked him if he remembered her from Toronto. He did, and gave her a hug. Then Rose told him about her gift. She pulled the blanket out of her bag, and cameras flashed all over the room! She explained that it was a gift from her heart, to the heart of the Backstreet Boys.

Later, there was a silent auction, and she discovered she was standing right beside Howie, literally rubbing sleeves with him! It was great!

As Rose was leaving that night she handed the blanket to Howie's assistant. The next day, they left the Big Apple. It had been a blast!

CHAPTER TEN

Finding Out Who
True Friends Are

R ose met a **Nick Carter fan,** in the MSN chat room, who had a lot in common with Rose. The fan's name was Angela Serafino, and she had spina bifida. Rose called her Angie for short and shared that she had lupus SLE and had met Nick through the Foundation. Angie was from Texas, was three years older than Rose, and had the same love for the Backstreet Boys. They hit it off immediately.

As Rose got to know her better, she learned that Angie had been engaged for a couple of years. She told Rose that she had had a dream about marrying Joe Mack from NKOTB, when she was only six years old! As she grew a bit older, she realized it would not happen. Then Angie saw Nick in his group on TV, and like all little girls do, she screamed to see such a good looking guy! So then, Angie became a fan of the BSB and Nick. They had this in common.

Just before Christmas, Rose reconnected with her old school crush. She decided to contact him and tell him how she had felt about him in Grade 8. His response really shook her. He replied, "I knew you had feelings for me, but you never said anything. I wasn't sure how to approach you, knowing I was the popular kid with asthma and you were someone without many friends." Rose did not know how to respond. As she thought about it, she figured he would not want to be with someone who had gone through as much, medically, as she had. She did not respond.

Rose's family had a huge Christmas/New Year's party. The house was full of guests. She fulfilled her role as hostess and made friends with two of the girls, Jocelyn and Alexia (Lexxie for short). She entertained them with movies on her computer and before they left, they exchanged emails so they could stay in touch. The three of them enjoyed close friendships.

In January, 2007, Rose found a blog. One aspect of the comments was about how people treat celebrities during public appearances. She decided to write her own opinion and was surprised when the owner of the blog contacted her and wanted to stay in touch. As usual, Rose did not realize that although she was 21, her thoughts were those of a much younger teenager. It was something that would always be an issue.

In February, two things happened. Rose experienced flu-like symptoms for two weeks. Then, as she was recovering, she learned what it was like to have a stroke. It was not Rose, but her mom who had a mini-stroke and had to be taken to ER by ambulance. Rose rode in the front seat. It was hard to believe they had switched places. Usually it was Rose on the stretcher and her mom watching. She stayed with her mom, the entire time in the ER. Something quite funny happened. Rose was wearing a dark blue tracksuit, and was mistaken as a nurse! Rose never left her mom's side, as Khem was going through all the tests. Luckily, her mom did not have to stay the night and they returned home. In the days to come, her mom had over forty tests done, to identify the problems. Khem had to wear a machine on her chest to monitor her heart rate, in case she had another stroke. And, there was another shocking result from the examinations. Khem had bone cancer.

Khem asked Rose to take her place at a seminar for the business. Rose tried to take notes, but could not concentrate. All she could think about was imagining life without her mom. She was crying her eyes out. She went home and crawled into bed with her mom, crying herself to sleep.

May 14, 2007
Dear Diary,

Hello, it's 10:30 pm. You won't believe who I have been talking to for the past month! I was able to talk to Nick Carter on the phone! I never thought it could happen. I have been using My Space I.M. I have become Nick's Princess, Nick's girl, Nick's babe, and his Best Friend. I feel so good right now!

May 15, 2007
Dear Diary,

I know it's late but I have big news. I actually talked to Britney Spears. She said that she, Katrina, European Boy Band and BSB are coming to visit me for Katrina's 18th birthday, on July 11 this year! I was close to bringing up my dinner from the excitement.

In terms of her health, Rose had her last does of prednisone on Friday, April 13, 2007. Great! When she went to her room that night, her heart nearly stopped when this photo of Nick Carter came to mind. She had to tell someone about her feelings for him. She knew she should have told Angie, right then. They understood each other's feelings for Nick.

Instead, Rose turned to the chat rooms in Europe, even though many of the members probably were not real. During the conversations, she did at least seven all-nighters. It was a wonder she could keep her act together, on any level.

Later, Rose received a message from a woman who was preparing a fundraiser for Lupus. She thought this was cool, so replied. Thus, a friendship with Trudy began. They shared about hobbies and became fast friends. Trudy was a mother in her thirties, who had a thyroid disorder. She had two children, Christopher and Megan. Trudy and her son Christopher were huge fans of the BSB: Trudy liked Howie D and Christopher liked Nick. Rose shared her experiences with Howie D, and Trudy shared her plans for a Lupus fundraiser. She asked Rose to help. Rose thought it was a good idea, since she could explain lots of her experiences.

Trudy invited Rose to come to her house for two and a half weeks. Rose thought it was a marvelous idea. But there was one fact that caused Rose's family to wonder if it was advisable: Trudy had a strong fear of the fictional character, "Jason". It was out of proportion. Nevertheless, Khem prepared a big feast and invited Trudy over to meet them. Trudy brought all her family, but excluded her own mother. They learned that she had recently moved in with her mother, since the lovely basement apartment they had been living in, formerly, had been flooded. This new house was from the 60's, only had three small bedrooms, one bathroom and an unfinished basement full of their belongings.

Rose was surprised how quickly she adapted, after she arrived in. But she had not been expecting the frequent, loud family fights, especially between Trudy and her mother. The mother screamed as loud as a full sports stadium! It became obvious the family did not agree with Trudy's idea for a Lupus fundraiser. It turned out, that Trudy had been asking for help from her family for the past year, and had not been receiving any. It was a complicated mess.

Sleeping arrangements were no better. Unfortunately, the spare bedroom was an office, so no sleeping there. Consequently, Trudy and her daughter slept on a medium sized thick mattress in the living room, Christopher slept on the couch, and Michael, the father, slept in the basement. Rose, of course, had to sleep in the living room beside Trudy and Megan!

Rose wondered how such an unorganized family could ever properly plan the event. And she hoped she did not end up in hospital, where she had never been before. Sure enough, her ankles and shoulders became itchy from fleas or bug bites and she had to be taken to ER. After that, she slept in the small trailer that was in the driveway.

Other issues included proper eating. There were stashes of food, but they were for a specific person. It was 'hands off'. Trudy did take her grocery shopping, but Rose had no idea where that food went. Christopher, or Trudy's brother, Carl, seemed to claim everything. They never asked if she was hungry or thirsty, or if she needed anything. Someone with Lupus needs a regular diet and regular rest. Neither was easy. One day, she was napping in the trailer, when Christopher banged loudly on the outside.

The event never did get well organized. And Rose was dealing with the psychological humiliation of receiving no care. Her mom called several times, but Rose did not want to let on how bad things were. Rose did research and found a lupus foundation cruise at the end of the year. She and Trudy agreed to share a cabin, if they went.

When Rose returned home, she acted as if everything was fine and did not let on how dysfunctional Trudy's family had been. She and Trudy kept in touch by phone or I.M.

Rose's mom then asked her if she would like to move to Laos, to live! Rose was concerned about the cost of her many medications and the quality of health care. She had enjoyed her two visits to the country, but did not speak the language. She thought that would be a huge barrier. She told her mom she would think about it.

Then the weekend of Trudy's event arrived. Rose went camping with her, expecting a bit of comfort. But they roughed it. She found it hard to even stay warm! And Trudy's husband, Michael, only decided to help, the night before! Then, they slept in! But they were still up by 6:30 am. In the mad scramble, Rose almost dumped her day's medications down the drain! Trudy managed to get the canopies set up on the beach. Even though the planning had not been great, the event did fairly well. They raised five hundred dollars.

Rose did her best to put on a good face. Fortunately, it was a nice day. As usual, food-wise, it was everyone for themselves. When Rose went to get food, and came back with enough for herself, Trudy's friend accused her of not thinking about anyone but herself. Rose decided not to even elaborate on how it felt to be called selfish, in that family's situation.

Throughout the day, it often felt as if Trudy forgot Rose was even there. Waking at 6:30 am, had left her exhausted and alone. It was a long day. Trudy's family may have refused to help with organizing the event, but they were more than ready to help clean up! And then there was finally pizza for supper.

You wouldn't believe where Rose ended up, after the fundraiser. Three days later her Stepfather had to take her to the ER with a temperature of 104.8 degrees. She knew it was because of what she had gone through, especially not drinking during the event. They were in ER for 8 hours! Rose talked to Trudy the next day and told her about her fever. Trudy did not express any concern or well wishes. All she did was ask Rose if she would help with the next Lupus event. Rose said she would think about, knowing full well, she would not go.

Last Good Cause and Deciding

After Khem was diagnosed with bone cancer, she was advised to go through chemotherapy. Instead, Khem decided to go back to Laos for alternative medicine. At the same time, Rose and Trudy were preparing their plans for going on the charity cruise. Trudy insisted she take a Greyhound bus to the port, while Rose's family wanted her to fly. It was a repeat of the stress of the event, all over again. Luckily, two friends she had met last year were also coming on the cruise! Her family won out, and she flew to the cruise port.

During the cruise, Rose hoped to chat with Howie D and find out any news about Nick. But once again, relationships interfered. Her group of five was divided up between 2 sleeping cabins. None of them got along, It was constant warfare, even to the point of disturbing nine other cabins, one night! The trip was a fiasco.

When Rose returned home, she ended up on the couch for two weeks, with fatigue, aches, pains, and light headedness. It was partly from stress, but also from the drastic change in temperature, from tropical to freezing. She had a sore diaphragm, and slept most of the time, even for Christmas and New Years. What a way to end the year.

Rose continued chatting with a variety of people, mostly from Europe. She always felt that most of them were fake, but enjoyed hearing them talk about their musical activities, anyways Fortunately, she remained friends with Angie, and they could always share their feelings about Nick.

Rose wanted to begin school again, since she had had to drop out during grade nine. Her Stepdad helped her enroll in an upgrading course, where adults could enhance their reading, writing, and math skills. She knew math was her weakest subject. Now she would have to wait and see if her health would cooperate.

CHAPTER ELEVEN

School, After Four Years

The **Literary Council allows adults to excel** in Reading, Writing and Math. Rose knew she was weak in Math and definitely wanted to update her skills. It was rewarding, because she soon moved up a Math class!

However, getting to school was a problem. At first, her stepdad had to drive her each day. There was public transit, but the last time she used it was years ago, when she and Jamie had traveled to school each day. Eventually, Rose did gain confidence, and traveled on her own, by bus. She found herself really enjoying each trip: wonderful accomplishment.

Most of the students attended the class because of some set-back or physical ailment. Rose got to know one of the students. He was a young guy who had a speech impairment. He explained his hopes of being with someone one day. She encouraged him that he would find someone special, one day.

At the end of the day, while everyone was just hanging out, he began to make teasing advances towards her. He moved closer and told her how nice she was. He asked her to be his girlfriend. She said, "No thank you", as politely as possible. She did not want to tell him that Nick was always on her mind.

On the bus, one day, another boy from class had down syndrome, had caught her eye, and said, "I would be a good guy to be with." Again, she politely declined.

Later, the boy that had down syndrome stopped right in front of her as he got off the bus, leaned over and attempted to kiss her. She was very shaken by this incident and reported it at school, when she arrived. When the school had a pizza party, she noticed he stayed far away from her. The staff must have spoken to him.

For the summer, Rose found a Tutor, who helped her with writing. The most important thing she learned was to avoid 'run-ons', sentences that had no end! The tutor helped her with essay writing. At first, neither of them could come up with a topic. Then the tutor emailed her with the suggestion of BSB and three of their songs. Rose thought this was ingenious! She chose these three songs: 'Show Me the Meaning of Being Lonely', 'Incomplete', and 'I Need You Tonight'. Of course, she enjoyed writing it since it was her favorite boy band!

That summer Rose attended two BSB concerts! Finally, it was better late than never. After all, she had been a fan since 1997! Her mom went with her to the first one. Rose made a sign that said, "Nick, I will Always Love U 4 Who U R. Forever, Nicksprincess". On it were two photos from the time she had met him, seven years earlier. But in the entrance line-up, as she chatted with other fans, one asked to see her sign. She did not want to open it until the show started, so she said, "Not yet". Her mother told her that was not nice, and one of the fans told her they hated her. It took away some of the excitement. She had also hoped to give Nick a gift, near the backstage. That did not work out either. When she got home, she mailed it, hoping she had the right address. It was still nice to be at the concert, though.

Rose submitted a piece of writing about her health, through the Literary Council, and it was published in a news article! She had begun writing her story, and a teacher suggested she hand in a brief version, with just the important facts about what she had gone through. It was rewarding to have it accepted!

As the summer continued with her tutor, Rose began to excel in her multiplication skills and even acquired the level of Math Wizard in a Multiplication Bingo game! Then, one day she was able to prove her tutor wrong in a word problem! Rose had always loved them, back in grade school. They sure had a good laugh over that one!

For the second BSB concert, Rose asked to stay with her cousin, who lived near the concert hall. She made another sign that said, "Nick, You Saved Me the Day We Met 02/26/03.' She made sure she hid it until the show started, this time. Rose had no idea if he saw it, because her seat was high up in the stands. It was still wonderful to be there. However, her mom dropped a bomb, on the way home in the car. Khem told her that would be her last experience with BSB. There was to be no more after this. Her family just did not understand what a motivational tool the BSB band was in her life.

Rose and Angie were still talking regularly. Their mutual admiration for the BSB kept them close friends. At one point, when they were talking about Rose's family's lack of understanding about her strong feelings, Angie suggested she write them a letter, explaining how she felt. Rose agreed and wrote one, storing it on her USB stick, instead of giving it to her family. She continued to update it over the years, often holding back her emotions of animosity towards her family.

On December 9, 2008, Rose's doctor told her she could stop taking five of her medications! Now she was down to two! At one time she had taken twenty-two pills, three times a day. It had taken six years of healing to reach this point.

Then Rose heard that Nick was having birthday parties in various locations around Canada! She asked her mom if she could attend one last event. Her mom agreed and got them tickets. Rose even emailed the manager asking for a few minutes to talk with Nick. Then when he stopped in front of her, she froze. She forgot she had her mom's phone to take a picture. Nick did wave at her a few times, throughout the evening. Her mom pushed her up to the front, but after she was elbowed a few times, she felt others thought she should not be there. She did get the manager to ask Nick to autograph a photo, but then she had to run from the building.

Her mom put the final damper on the evening, by talking, on the way home, about finding love and getting a rich boyfriend in Laos. "That is it for the BSB; no more. You need to come home with your mom, to Laos, and find a rich boyfriend and be happy. You don't need someone like Nick Carter, who doesn't even know you exist." When they got home, her brother Jamie agreed with their mom. It was a bad ending to what should have been a great evening.

To make matters worse, Rose found a video of Nick with his hand laced through the hand of a brunette, but she chose to forget about it.

Back at school, Rose was achieving! She moved from upgrading, to a normal classroom! As an adult, she was completing her education! Rose was learning how to do a PowerPoint slideshow. She accomplished it in one day and her stepdad told her she was a quick learner when it came to new things. What a great compliment!

On her 23rd birthday, her mom took the family to a mandarin restaurant, to celebrate. It was a wonderful day!

Rose's first assignment was a media project. What would be her topic? Her teacher said to do it on something that made her comfortable. Immediately, drugs and alcohol popped into her mind. When she began researching, she discovered there was far more information on drugs, so that was her choice. It seemed logical, too, since she had been taking so many drugs, and they were not the street kind.

However, shocking news about Nick slightly altered her topic. On a Facebook group entitled 'Support Nick Carter', Rose learned that Nick had a heart condition called cardiomyopathy. Nick had an enlarged heart and had been experiencing chest pains since the spring of 2008. She bought 'The Exclusive People Magazine', and read the whole story. She could identify with being diagnosed with a serious illness. She understood what he was going through. It was relieving to read that he had caught the problem early enough. So, the project focused on drugs taken by Nick and other celebrities. Unfortunately, she discovered how many stars were addicted to drugs and often passed away under the influence. How could actors, actresses, and singers, who seemed so smart, go for something so dumb? It was a revelation to realize Nick had taken drugs, and not just for medicinal purposes.

Rose produced a slide show and flyers on the celebrities who she researched. She got 68% on her midterm report, despite being sick and missing a week of school in the term. She was pleased that she kept working at the assignment, even when she was ill.

Rose was quite nervous during her presentation of the project. She had not done public speaking since elementary school. She was able to keep her emotions under control and earned 75% for her final mark. Great going!

Rose came to realize she had a tendency to overwork. She went at things vigorously, without a break. And her brain had a habit of showing her ten different ideas at once. Many of them were not actually relevant to the task. She had to learn to focus on the necessary process.

So, until the end of June, Rose attended school full time. The upgraded math class was two hours in the morning, and then there was a half-hour break for lunch, followed by the two-hour literacy class. It was a full schedule but she could handle it!

During this time Rose still kept in touch with Angie. Since Angie's fiancé had passed away, Rose did her best to help her, emotionally. Then she discovered Angie had begun a relationship with someone new. Rose wondered if it was too soon, but she really had no idea.

At this time, Rose made a twitter account and found Nick's account. She discovered a girl's name connected to it and began searching for all his past girlfriends. She was not impressed with the information about the girl he was with and hoped he did not get hurt. But finding a site to order a BSB hoodie helped a lot! She only took if off to wash it!

Rose's time at the Adult Learning Centre was well spent. Her overall average in Math was not great; it was 56%. But on her last test she got 96%! It involved doing five exams and was worthwhile.

Then Rose decided to sign up for summer classes. She took Workplace Math, since she was not planning on continuing on to College. She also attended the Senior class. However, things became confusing and she was caught copying. Her program coordinator advised that she forget about school, since it was difficult for her to handle. It ended up being a year off. Rose had also interrupted writing her health story. She put it on hold temporarily.

Moving on, Rose invited a boy she had met in class, and his dad, out to a business meeting. It turned out the father was not interested, but the boy asked her out for lunch and a movie. They saw the movie Avatar, at the theatre in the same building as the Learning Centre. It was her second time seeing it, but she did not mention that. Then he took her home to meet his parents. His dad drove her home. She was not sure how she felt, being with the boy.

It was discouraging, not being able to graduate with her grade twelve diploma. But she got into volunteering, and turned it into hours of community service. Rose was thankful her stepdad had helped her get into the school, even though the administrators had told her to forget it, at the end. She still had the ambition to complete her grade twelve, some day.

That summer, she turned back to her crafts. Rose made another blanket, with information about Nick written on it. She also completed a dolphin puzzle she had begun in 2003 when she was on the feeding tube. She sent these two items, with a letter, off to Nick, hoping she had the correct address. At this time, Rose began writing a novel about a girl with a love interest that was impossible. It actually made her depressed, because no one understood her feelings for Nick, a person who was way beyond reach.

CHAPTER TWELVE

Writer's Club

While Rose was wondering about school, she found a local writer's club, which could offer advice to new writers. She wanted to find a publisher who was interested in her health story. This might enable her to see Nick again.

Since Rose had been writing her story for over three years, she definitely had material to bring, for consideration. It would be her non-fiction rather than her fiction writing. Probably the others would not be interested in fiction stories about a girl being with a celebrity. This theme would probably not bode well with the other writers in the club.

Rose soon met a fellow writer who owned a car and she asked for a ride home. Soon they were hanging out together. Of course, it became awkward because she was avoiding mentioning Nick.

However, when they discussed her health story, the subject of Nick invariably came up, and she explained how she felt about him.

Then Rose invited him to watch a video, to see if he was interested in joining her family's business. At the end, he was looking at her, not the video. She knew he was interested in her more than in the business.

Another night, the writer asked Rose to go to the movie 'Avatar' with him. She had the feeling he was going to ask her to be his girlfriend. Sure enough, as the car warmed up, after the show, he held her hands to help her warm up and told her what a nice girl she was. "Will you be my girlfriend?" Rose asked for three weeks to think about it. He replied, "You are going to end up alone if you keep your feelings about Nick Carter."

When she got home, Rose was so stressed that even her feet were numb. As she warmed up, she talked with her mom, who wanted to know how the evening had gone. Khem was disappointed Rose had let a male friend go, once again, because of Nick. She wanted to know when Rose was going to realize Nick would never be interested in her. To change the subject, Rose brought up the subject of living in Laos, as if she wanted to move overseas.

The next morning, Rose paced around and around the house, looking out to the spot where the writer's car had been parked last night. Her mom asked if she was in love with him. Rose refused to answer and instead began working on a fiction story from last year. From that point on, she had her stepdad drive her to writer's club.

Just before Easter, her doctor allowed her to stop taking Lisinopril. It was great! Unfortunately, she did have to go back to it, later, since her kidneys were still losing protein. But the temporary rest, was nice.

At Easter, Bob came for a BBQ. While Rose and her mom were outside, they began talking and her mom suggested she go to live in Laos, or with her dad in Milwaukee. Rose immediately brought up how her dad had hurt her so badly when she was seven. Her mom was shocked that she still remembered. Rose asked if either Bob or Jamie knew about it and Khem said it would make them very angry. Rose asked her to tell Bob. The result: their Easter dinner was burned, and Rose was blamed!

From that point on, Rose immersed herself in writing romance novels. As well, she was using social media, a lot, until her accounts were hacked. So she withdrew for about nine months, until Bob encouraged her to return, but just with friends she knew. Rose also continued doing her volunteer community service at the local library. She was thrilled to discover she was over the 40 hours, required for Grade 12!

Another time Rose was at a venue for the Back Street Boys. She wanted to get a note to Nick, and tried several methods. Just as she was about to give up, Rose noticed one of the wives, LeighAnne, who agreed to take the note and to have her picture taken with Rose. After the show, she purchased a photo of Nick from a 2003 tour! Rose sure appreciated her parents driving her to and from the event. It was a wonderful evening.

Bob invited Rose to his condo for Christmas! It was wonderful and she was able to meet his girlfriend and her family. The girlfriend's father told her he wanted the first copy of her published book! What an encouragement.

Unfortunately, Rose's mom became very sick, during a trip to Laos. During the week of Rose's twenty-fifth birthday, Khem had to go to ER three times. Fortunately, Khem recovered well. At the same time, Rose took a stab at teaching her class about her health. She had fun. At this time, Rose was buying a lot of BSB souvenirs, and her mom had to tell her to slow down on spending money.

During the holiday, Rose also began to feel that something bad was about to happen to Nick. Her feelings increased, while she was busy doing another essay. Later that week, she read that news that one of Nick's younger siblings had passed away. It was his sister, Leslie, who was only a few months younger than Rose. It was a shock and Rose felt very sad for Nick and his family. She posted condolences on Facebook, but was mocked by her oldest brother and his girlfriend. From then on, she did not talk about Nick in front of her family.

A week later, Rose felt psychologically drained by her present situation. She ended up at a clinic, explaining to a doctor that she needed to see a psychologist or a therapist to talk about things she could not talk to her mother about. She was given a prescription for an anti-depressant, instead, but did not take them. Another week later, Rose contacted the Guidance Counselor and was given the advice to try College, rather than bothering with Grade Twelve. This did not have a good ending, but more about that later.

Next, Rose sent a care package to Nick. In it were her written poems. A month later it returned, at her expense; forty dollars for nothing. Her mom suggested she write Ellen Degeneres, explaining why she wanted to be a guest, to meet Nick and the Back Street Boys. She wrote a couple of times but received no reply. So, instead, she wrote a short fiction story about it, *"The Biggest Reunion in History"*.

Rose was still attending a writer's club, but her feelings about her family were beginning to show. One night, her emotions were so strong, the founder suggested Rose should get some help. Rose went to the nearest mental health association) with the document she had received from Child Services. She explained her feelings about her mom. Soon she had a Social Worker. After a particularly difficult session, she was distraught, and asked to be taken to ER. During this appointment, her older brother offered to have her come and spend a week with him and his girlfriend, for a short time away from her mom. However, they both kept advising her to figure out how to deal with her issues, to get a job, to be with someone, etc. They were not helping.

During March break, Rose was invited to visit the family of her old high school boy friend. It was a wonderful get together. The mother had always thought she was an orphan, because her family had never been around. When the mother heard that she had not spoken to Jane since 2006, she suggested Rose call Jane and have a long talk. She said the cost did not matter. So Rose talked to Jane for three hours! What a connection!

When she returned, Rose got right into her last assignment for her course. She had to shadow someone in her career choice. She followed an ER nurse, from 10 am to 5 pm and filled out the response booklet. It was a great way to end her course.

In May, Rose began looking for an apartment. Her mom helped her find a place two blocks from the family. This allowed her to visit the a Festival. She introduced herself to radio announcers and asked them to play Back Street Boys songs. It was a pleasant outing.

CHAPTER THIRTEEN

Taste of Independence

Rose moved into her own apartment! It was behind a commercial building. It was a single unit, but plenty big enough for one person. She spent most of the first month, settling in. Of course, the first thing she did was put up here BSB posters. The group photos were in the main living area, while Nick's were in the bedroom. Her favourite was the group photo with them all dressed in black, laying in a circle. It was wonderful arranging her own place.

During that summer of 2012, Rose also hung out in a restaurant where she was with the radio announcer who was filling in while another announcer, who was a big BSB fan, was on vacation. The replacement announcer reminded her of Nick.

On the last Friday of the summer she met all of the announcers and had her picture taken with them. She felt very happy, being friends with the local radio announcers of the city of

Barrie. Whenever she had pictures taken with them at events she always gave the spare to the evening announcer who reminded her of Nick! Rose even added the announcers on Facebook, to keep in contact with them. Whenever they played a BSB tune, she would endorse the post, both for the station and for the band.

By the end of August, when Rose had been living independently in her apartment for three months, she began researching magazine editors and publishers, to get her story out there. As well, she went out nearly every day to explore the downtown area. She bumped into her friend in the wheelchair, and they had good times, catching up. It was great freedom.

Rose was still in contact with Angie. They wondered if Nick would propose to his girlfriend. It made Rose think about her feelings for Nick, and to remember the first time she tried to contact him, in 2004. She realized Nick was not able to be concerned with how fans felt about him. It was hard not to be able to share her life with him. She wrote many short stories with titles such as: Come to Me, Public Display of Affection, and Won't Give Up.

The first week of September she received an email from a local magazine, stating she could send in in some of her written work. Then a publishing company in the States called. Then the local radio station called about her entry in a contest. She correctly answered, "B101 plays Barrie's Hit Music." Imagine her surprise when the announcer replied with, "Hello Rose!" She had won! She chatted with the afternoon announcer until she had to go back on the air. Then her call was broadcast on the air waves!

Rose was half-way through her life story, but she couldn't seem to go any further. It was at the point where she first met Nick Carter, and her feelings prevented her from proceeding. No matter how many times she tried, she became entirely frustrated and could not continue. How was she going to get it ready for either of the publishers who had contacted her?

Then another incident slowed down her writing. In October of 2012, she connected with her grade three teacher, from School in town. The last time they had spoken was when Rose was being told she had to repeat grade three. That talk had stayed with Rose for a long time. But now, ten years later, she began planning a visit town. She hadn't been there since 1999.

The teacher and Rose made plans for her to go up north and visit for about a week. She could catch up with friends and faculty members from her old schools. Rose could also fill in her teacher about her life since moving in 1999. However, when she shared these plans with her family, the reaction was not great. Her older brother was even afraid she might decide to stay in town, where life can be pretty boring. Rose was not deterred, and hopped on the bus.

Her first task was to try and get in touch with Jane. None of the numbers she had worked. No one seemed to know anything.

Her second was to visit her old High School, where she asked if it would be possible to return and finish her education. It would not work, for two reasons. First, she needed her files from the Learning Centre. She had not thought to get them. Secondly, where would she live? Better give up on that idea. But she enjoyed going around and seeing her former teachers.

Thirdly, she stopped at, her elementary school. She said hello to the secretary. The last time they had seen each other was at the 50th birthday celebration Rose had attended with her parents. Then the next person Rose ran into was the lunchroom supervisor who used to give her a hard time during lunch period. This time, however, they had a nice chat and caught up on school news.

Several people asked if she had spoken with Jane. It always brought Rose close to tears. So her mom's friend suggested they go to her house and see if Jane was home. What they discovered came as a big shock. Jane no longer lived there. Then they went to Rose's old childhood house the present occupants had completely remodelled the house. Rose's bedroom was now the laundry, the master bedroom had a walk-In closet, there was a pantry in the kitchen, the basement was being transformed into a fitness room, and the second basement bedroom had become a bathroom. In her opinion, the house had been destroyed. No memories were left.

Rose's next visit was with old friends her parents had known since arriving in Canada from Laos. One of them was now 80 but still going strong. Rose also visited with the two daughters. Rose had been named after them! They asked her to share about her life since leaving town. Of course, when she mentioned Nick it was hard to hold back the tears. The word 'obsessed' did come up. It was also difficult to discuss her mother's past involvement with the internet based business, while she had lived in town. Rose knew her mom would want a full report, and some of the discussions were quite negative.

Now it was time to visit her grade three teacher, who still lived across from the Catholic Church. Rose remembered her embarrassing fall, there, after grade eight graduation. It was great to catch up as friends, no long teacher and student. Rose was pretty much able to explain most of the ordeal, from the time her family left town in 1997, to the present. Then the teacher took her to Mass on Sunday, where Rose connected with more friends from her past. Rose and the teacher went out for breakfast, and talked a little more. Great get-together.

Many people encouraged Rose to make an effort to locate Jane. She found another possible number and copied down the info. Then she boarded the bus for home, to her apartment in Barrie.

Now, Rose did not want to upset her mom, when she visited her after the trip. But her mom wanted to know everything the town folks had said about her doing business, especially with the internet based business, all the time, then and now. Rose had to be honest and say many of them questioned where the profits were going. Khem reacted strongly and wanted to know how Rose had answered them. It blew up into an unpleasant argument, just as Rose had known it would. Rose gave vague answers, trying to avoid the conversation. As her mom drove Rose back to her apartment, the car was thick with tension. Khem's last response was calling Rose an ungrateful child. Rose did not know what to say. They were both in tears.

CHAPTER FOURTEEN

3rd and Last to Finish

Rose wanted to find out about the credits she still needed to graduate. She spoke with the guidance counsellor at the Learning Centre and discovered she could finish by taking one more course! A week later, Rose was visiting with her stepdad, while her mom was on her annual trip to Laos. During the visit, she received a call confirming she would start class on December 4th and be finished by January 29th, the day after Nick's birthday. That meant she would be free from the end of January, until the graduation ceremony.

Rose worked hard on the course, Environmental Science. One humorous incident involved a video by Rick Mercer that the teacher was showing in class. Mr. Mercer was investigating what it would be like to be the person who picked up recycling. Near the end, he went to the recycling depot. Rose noticed a stereo system and could not help commenting that someone was throwing away a BSB cassette! She made sure she sent that YouTube link to Angie!

The course involved writing six assignments. Rose finished them by Christmas, so she could celebrate the Christmas holiday and the arrival of 2013 without schoolwork. She relaxed, but continued writing, and also made plans to visit Angie in the future.

The publishing company contacted Rose. Her contact had been promoted and the replacement was a lovely girl who was a fan of Nick's younger brother, Aaron. It felt good to tell her that she planned to send her writing during 2013. She might become a published author, before she became an adult High School graduate.

Rose's excitement built as she finished her schooling in January. When she entered her apartment at the end of the last day, her eyes went straight to the poster of the group in black laying in a circle, and she exclaimed, "I'm done!"

Rose began to think about graduation, and inviting Nick and the group. Her feelings for Nick had become stronger over the years. During this time, living in her apartment, she did not pay attention to her health. Her mind was on graduation, not medication, and on being with Nick, as part of the BSB family. Nothing else mattered.

So imagine the shock, when Facebook announced that Nick had asked the brunette 'the question'! She sat in her computer chair for an hour, feeling like her world had come to an end. She wrote one more story and then could not focus on anything. The story was about Nick and Rose planning and singing a concert together. The fans got to know who Rose was and loved everything about her, just like the other BSB wives. Then she sank into depression.

Rose began posting her frustration on Facebook, not caring if people thought she was crazy. Even messages from her mom and Jamie did not stop her lengthy posts. She wondered if anyone would care if she ended her life.

Fortunately, the publishing company contacted her and suggested she finish her life story. She had only covered events from 2001 to 2009. So Rose was encouraged to add the last five years, to complete the book.

Easter that year was full of difficulties. Rose received a twitter from Nick's girlfriend, telling her to leave her fiancé alone. There was a lot more to the message, but Rose did not read it. She blocked it. Then, during Easter dinner at her brother's, she could not hide her feelings. Her family all wanted to know what was wrong. It was difficult to explain how she felt like Nick was all she needed in her life.

To distract herself, Rose began watching action movies. She had a marathon of non-stop Steven Seagul movies. She also discussed moving back home, with her mom. She had loved living independently, until Nick made his announcement. It had been wonderful being a loyal fan, not some crazy teen, yelling her head off and jumping up and down when she heard their music. They were amazingly sweet and talented, especially Nick. All she wanted was a few minutes of their time.

April 20, 2013 was the twentieth anniversary of the BSB. They would be receiving a Star on the Walk of Fame. They also hosted a fan celebration. Problems with the live feed prevented Rose from seeing the first half.

In May, a writer friend invited Rose out for dinner. She went with her to the meeting of the writer's club, but didn't stay long. She could not focus. Then Rose helped her friend in a wheelchair, by being with her in the hospital. The friend was also having emotional problems over a love interest. The month was turning out to be quite a bumpy ride. Another incident involved finally contacting Jane. They caught up on each other's news, but Jane would not commit to coming down for graduation. That was possibly her last call to Jane. Another downer.

At the end of May, Rose moved back home. Her book was on the verge of being published, and Jamie was coming home from Laos, for the summer and her graduation. Her mom suggested a good title for her book: "If Life Gave Me Lemons, I

Would Turn It into Honey." Her mom complimented Rose by saying she had turned her challenges into something good and sweet. She gave the all clear to print the book, even though it did not seem all the editing had been done. Then, throughout the summer, she dealt with promoting the book and handling Jamie's constant critiques.

For her graduation, Rose chose sushi as her preferred dining place. Unfortunately, Jamie did not like that, so they ended up going to a different restaurant for her stepfather instead. She was disappointed she did not even get that choice.

Near the end of the summer, Rose went to see her social workers, to update them on what had been happening in her life over the last year. They advised her not to dwell on whether or not Nick had anything to do with sending her the tweet. They then guided her to a place for counselling. She attended the walk-in clinic at Catholic Family Life, regularly, after that. After each visit, she was able to go home and work on writing for a while. However, the appointments were every two weeks, and the motivation did not last long, after each visit. The rest of the time, she watched Fast & Furious movies. She also deactivated her Facebook account. She did not delete it, in case she decided to return.

Rose's walk-in sessions changed to ongoing sessions, enabling her to have six more sessions, once a week. It was good to be able to continue.

Rose's mom made suggestions for her book. She thought Rose should tell how the business had helped her throughout her life. Her mom read positive motivational books, listened to audios, and showed the business plan whenever she could. She could not seem to understand that Rose did not feel the same way, after the episode in 1995. Rose wished her mom would realize how much it had hurt her, and apologize. But her mom had no clue. At Christmas, they all talked about it, and her mom did say she was sorry. For Rose, though, it seemed that the business was always more important than Rose.

The week before Christmas in 2013, Rose went in for a kidney biopsy. She had lost more protein than she should have. The intake nurse thought she was a fan of NKOTB. She had to tell her it was BSB, instead. But she was able to give her a copy of her book. Imagine her surprise when the doctor commented, as he was starting the biopsy, "You have an amazing personality, but bad taste in music!"

At this point in her life, Rose really did not care what happened to her. If her health declined, it did not matter. Even though her parents were worried about what she went through, she knew she would never get what she wanted in life.

By New Year, Rose was close to finishing her second book, "Life to SLE – A Documentary". It was a lot more detailed than the first book. She was also working on a brand new knitting project, 'The Future of the Backstreet Family'. It had all the original members with the wives. Of course, she put her name in the place of someone else's. She felt like she was one of them, at least mentally. She would always think of herself as part of the Backstreet Family.

Printed in the United States
By Bookmasters